What My Sister Told Me After She Was Murdered

A Shared Journey of Transformation

What My Sister Told Me After She Was Murdered

First Printing March 2024

Ebook - ISBN: 979-8-9921498-0-7
Paperback - ISBN: 979-8-9921498-1-4

Library of Congress Control Number: TXu 2-384-629
Printed in the United States of America

Cover Photo - reddoorknoxville.com

What My Sister Told Me After She Was Murdered

A Shared Journey of Transformation

A True Story
by Annie Lisa

To my two favorite girls:

Mom, I'm so glad I chose you. Your unconditional love and strength have been the one constant in my life.

Tre, here's to all the magic we've shared and all that's yet to come.

An Unforgettable Journey Beyond the Veil

So compelling, I couldn't put it down!

In *What My Sister Told Me After She Was Murdered*, Annie Lisa takes us on an extraordinary ride, unraveling a story where love, loss, and unbreakable bonds transcend even death.

Guided by her sister—a renowned doctor who now resides on the Other Side of the Veil—Annie reveals how Spirit never stops communicating, especially when the stakes are as high as solving a murder. From the very first page, you're immersed in the clues, messages, and undeniable connection that lead these sisters to uncover the truth.

This isn't just a story about solving a crime—it's a profound lesson in how the bonds of love endure beyond this life. If you're curious about communication from the Other Side or simply love a gripping read, *What My Sister Told Me After She Was Murdered* is a must!

Highly recommend!
Kellee White, Spiritual Medium & Psychotherapist
Author of *Cracked Open*

INTRODUCTION

Every day for the last five years, I have heard a voice in my head. It always asks the same question, "When are you going to write the book?" At first it was a gentle, coaxing voice. But after months without so much as a sentence from me, the voice grew louder and impatiently commanded me, "You need to write the book!"

I knew it was my dead sister pestering me in death the same way she did when she was alive. Yet every time I heard her, I would answer silently, "I know. I know!"

Aside from being a professional procrastinator, I had every excuse in the world not to sit down and write, legitimate reasons, in fact. My sister and forever soulmate, Teresa, was brutally murdered, and I was raising her two orphaned children.

How's that for an excuse?

Prior to this, I considered myself a successful copywriter, and my family complimented the odd poem I wrote here and there, some of them pretty good. I had started to write a book about fifteen years ago, but I never finished it. Teresa used to harass me regularly about my inaction.

"So what are you doing?" she'd call to ask me on Sunday afternoons. This was her code for, "Are you being productive?" I would generally tell her that I was lying on my sofa watching a Lifetime movie. "Really? Well maybe you should get off your ass and finish that book you've been working on for the last seven years."

I continued to procrastinate, which drove my taskmaster of a sister completely nuts. That's how I knew it was my dead sister nagging me now to write *this* book.

Granted, she did cut me some slack, initially, because I had my hands full. One minute I was living a carefree, simple life with my husband, Petr, and my grown son, Mick, in my home—the old Victorian house I had grown up in and loved so much. I had a fruitful career and was lead singer in a blues band with one of my closest friends. My life was pretty fun and easy.

Then, in virtually the blink of an eye, it was all over. Before I knew it, I was living in a new, six thousand-square-foot carbon footprint home in the country with two traumatized kids and fancy landscaping. It was like turning the *Titanic* around in two seconds—my life changed that quickly.

***

At first it was a shock. My sister was dead? I didn't think I'd heard my brother correctly when he phoned me at work that Monday afternoon. And then four hours later, my shock grew to terror when I overheard my other brother solemnly answer his phone and then immediately start screaming to me what he had just heard on the other end of the phone from our brother, Frank: our sister Teresa was murdered.

Three days later, in unforgivable ignorance, I tightly embraced and consoled the man who had bludgeoned my sister to death with a hammer. "Thank you for being there for Mark and the kids." I wonder what he thought when I said that. I'm guessing he hoped that I'd never find out he'd murdered my sister.

So why, you're probably wondering, did Teresa expect me to write a book in the midst of all that chaos? Well, we had some unfinished business, a mission that we needed to complete. We understood this mission after receiving an epic message followed by a series of bizarre coincidences. All this occurred nine months to the day before her murder—a gestational metaphor that did not escape me. In fact, it underscored the profundity of our mission. The only problem was we didn't know exactly what we were supposed to do or how it would unfold, only that we were supposed to support humanity in a profound way. Now, with Teresa dead, I was left to figure everything out on my own—or at least that's what I thought at first.

My dead sister is a master at getting messages to me.

She does it with the same humor and no-nonsense approach she had in life. I've had my share of experiences talking to dead people, but there was no dead person I knew who had anything on Teresa. She was kicking ass and taking names from the other side. And she was naming names too—of people who didn't want to be named.

Like the name of the person who'd killed her.

Never one to waste time, and after the murder trials were finally over, Teresa was on to her next order of business. Even in death she would continue to make sure that I was living up to my potential, which largely meant pursuing our mission. She wanted me to pick up where we had left off. Only I didn't know what to do.

So I went back to the beginning and remembered how it all started.

About twenty-five years ago, I noticed that departed loved ones found profound ways to let me know they'd heard me talking to them. I'm not talking about seeing a random butterfly and thinking it was my Uncle Jeff, or that a cardinal with every right to be singing in my yard was most certainly my father—well, except maybe for the time I did see four of them gathered in a circle outside my studio shortly after he died. I'm talking about dynamic experiences that stop you in your tracks. The kind you can't write off as "just a coincidence." The kind that make the skeptic scratch his head and struggle to find a logical explanation.

I began to realize that reality was far more expansive than I ever thought possible.

All over the planet magical things are happening. Things we have been told are crazy and impossible. Past life regressions that offer insight into the issues we are struggling with in our current life. Or psychic mediums providing irrefutable proof that they are connecting to a departed loved one with specific information that only their living loved one could possibly know. People who've had near-death experiences, left their physical bodies, and then are able to recount details happened far beyond their hospital beds.

Yet we have to do our own digging to read about such phenomena. Okay, occasionally a random story such as a child remembering a past life as a World War II pilot has crossed the airways, but often with the media journalist speaking in a condescending tone and giving the audience a sideways glance suggesting you must be "cuckoo la-la" if you believe this.

I don't want to alienate the atheists or offend the theists. But can't we all agree that there is something much bigger happening beyond this three-dimensional reality that we perceive with our five senses?

We've been taught that if we can't understand something or explain how it works, then it must not be real. I can't explain how the internet works, and yet I don't think I'm being hyperbolic when I suggest that we practically worship it. Can you imagine trying to explain the internet to the people of Jamestown in 1640?

Even as recent as the nineteenth century, despite publicized results that hand-washing reduced mortality to below 2 percent, Ignaz Semmelweis's observations conflicted with the established scientific and medical opinions of the time. Eventually, Ignaz was committed to a sanitarium for the mentally insane. Ignaz was "cuckoo la-la."

Today, the most brilliant minds in the world still can't seem to figure out how the Universe works, but not for lack of trying. Through much study, research, and experimentation, quantum physicists believe the physical world that we perceive is not something that's separate from us, but rather created by our minds as we observe it.

What? I know what you're thinking. How are we responsible for the sad state of humanity? And how are we supposed to fix it?

And that brings me to the heart of this story.

We are responsible. We did create it. And my dead sister told me how we can fix it.

Are you ready?

CHAPTER 1

Journey's End

If there was one thing that frightened my sister, it was going home to an empty house, especially late at night. But that's what Teresa was about to do at 11:00 p.m. on June 28, 2015. No doubt she was exhausted after having traveled from Florida to spend two nights with her family in Connecticut. Sharing a house with your entire family and your siblings' families can do that to you. But soon she would dive into the comfort of her Tempur-Pedic® mattress that she loved so much. She needed a good night's sleep. Tomorrow was to be a big day. She was about to sign with a PR agency that would help her become a brand, "Dr. Teresa Sievers," the brilliant, no-nonsense doctor with a quick sense of humor.

Dr. Teresa Sievers was about to turn Western medicine upside down and open herself to sharp scrutiny. After all, there weren't too many board-certified medical doctors who promoted energy healing over prescription drugs. And if they did, they probably kept that under wraps, fearing ridicule from their colleagues. But Teresa didn't care what other people thought. She wasn't afraid to speak up. Teresa was all about the truth.

At any cost.

She was probably singing along with Mary J. Blige at full volume as she pressed the button on her car visor and watched the garage door open to her house that was for the neighborhood. I could just see her pointing her finger in the air and shaking her head back and forth as she sang along with M.J.

In a moment, she would step out of her vehicle, anticipating frenzied barking from her two dogs. Teresa could return from a twenty-minute trip to the grocery store, and those dogs would carry on at the other side of the door that led from the garage into the laundry room as if she'd abandoned them for a week.

But there was silence.

"Where the fuck are my dogs?" surely screamed through her mind and set her heart pounding. She might have calmed herself with thoughts of her security system for a second or two, until the hair began to stand up on the back of her neck. Why didn't she call me? Why didn't she call me! She had to have known that something was off. She had to!

She had to have sensed the presence of someone hiding in the dark.

He was just a few feet away, crouched behind her husband's motor-cycle, holding a hammer in his hand.

Chapter 2

The Beginning of the End

"Wait a minute! You never told me I could have butter," I shouted incredulously at my sister. For the last four years, my sister Teresa, a well-known and beloved doctor in Southwest Florida, had been sharing her wealth of knowledge with me on what to eat and what not to eat. And dairy was off limits. And now all of a sudden, I was allowed to have butter? What? How could she not tell me this?

Teresa had been telling me what to do since she was old enough to talk. It had always been that way, and somehow, I just accepted it. There was an innate knowing within me that she always knew best. Otherwise, why would I, at twelve years old, ask my then seven-year-old sister to help me with my homework, give me advice with boyfriend problems, and ponder the mysteries of the Universe? Because Teresa seemed to know everything. She personified the adage "an adult in a child's body." And like me, the rest of my family just accepted it.

Although unspoken, we all relied on Teresa to tell us what to do.

We were relaxing poolside on comfy lounge chairs on the last weekend of June 2015 in a house we had rented for our entire family to celebrate our mother's seventy-fifth birthday. We wanted to throw a party for Mom, but she protested, "All I want for my birthday is a weekend with my kids." In all, we were fifteen people: my older brother Patrick and his two children; my younger brother Frankie, his girlfriend, and his daughter; Teresa, her husband Mark, and their two kids; my mother and her husband Tom; and, of course, I was there with my husband Petr and my son, Mick. With the exception of my son, who was 19 at the time, the rest of my nieces and nephews were between eight and ten years old.

It wasn't just anxiety over butter substitutes that might have led to my unshapely downfall; it was that Teresa forgot to tell me. This was the most unsettling. It was so out of character. But in truth, it was a sign of what had been going on over the prior few months.

Teresa had been working tirelessly to integrate energy healing into her already expanded functional medical practice. She saw that when her patients reconciled with their stress and released emotional wounds, she could assist them with their body's innate wisdom to heal itself. Her approach to Western medicine was so refreshing that it wasn't long before word was out about Dr. Teresa Sievers. People started coming from all over to meet this one-of-a-kind doctor with a passion for getting them well.

Teresa was starting to get noticed by the local media. But she wanted more. "I'm wasting my fucking time looking down people's throats and up their asses."

Let me warn you. My sister loved to swear. I mean she *really* loved to swear. It was a personal art form that she had perfected. She could string together curse words and trash talk, turning them into parts of speech that one would never have imagined possible. And she did it so quickly and effortlessly that you had to be impressed more than offended, even if you were at the receiving end of her wrath.

Teresa was a paradox of hyperbolic proportions. She had the heart of Mother Teresa and a mouth like a truck driver—apologies to non-cursing truck drivers everywhere. Compassionate and kind she helped the homeless get housing and volunteered at a local foster home one minute, and then mercilessly cussed out staff if they let her down at the office the next. But that was Teresa. Yet her kindness and generosity made up for her lack of patience.

"People need to understand they are making themselves sick with their emotions and that they have the power to heal themselves," she'd lecture me, stomping around her kitchen with her hot rollers flopping around her head. "I can't do it one patient at a time. It takes too long. I want to reach the masses."

And that is exactly what she began doing. She started booking speaking engagements with anyone who would have her. She spoke at health food stores, connected with other businesses; she didn't care, as long as she could get people to understand the connection between their emotions and their well-being.

Teresa started to gain popularity and notoriety. She was filming a television show tentatively for DR TV. In fact, she had an appointment with a PR company scheduled for the day after she returned from our family vacation.

But she never made that appointment.

With a busy medical practice, volunteer work, two kids, and a husband who had finally gotten on her last nerve, Teresa was exhausted and exasperated. Nonetheless, she was unstoppable. But lately she had been so busy we'd barely had time to talk.

I missed our morning phone calls while we drank coffee and applied our makeup—hers naturally organic and of the highest quality, and mine a close second, aside from a few select pieces Teresa splurged on for me whenever we were together. Since she lived in Florida, while I remained in Connecticut living in the same house we grew up in, our morning phone call was a daily ritual that made us feel like we still lived close to each other. We didn't want to miss out on the day-to-day. When we were kids, we stood together in front of the same bathroom vanity, applying much less expensive make-up as we got ready for school. We went back in time on those morning calls before we left for work, chatting away as if we were in the same room. It was the best part of my day. And since these times had been so few lately, I was anxious for the chance to catch up with her on this family weekend.

But Teresa was off. Something was wrong. I could see her wheels spinning as she sat there twirling her hair. Thinking. She was thinking hard. She was about to figure something out. Something big. Something scary. And she was almost there, but not quite. I had seen this look on her face many times before.

When we were kids, we often overheard my mother and stepfather having an argument—private conversations or bits and pieces of screaming matches. Teresa and I hid in our bedroom, ears pressed to the door trying to hear what the argument was about and more importantly how it would impact our lives. I threw out guesses, "Are we in trouble? Do you think they are getting divorced? But Teresa, who was only six at the time, just sat there, twirling her hair and thinking, not really hearing me. All of a sudden she'd jump up on her bed and yell, "I've got it!" And then very confidently solve the latest mystery at hand.

That's what Teresa was like the last weekend I saw her alive—the same little girl about to jump on the bed.

Chapter 3

That Teresa

I was five and a half years old when my sister Teresa was born on November 19, 1968. My mom had gone into labor in the middle of the night. When I walked downstairs that morning from my bedroom in the tiny Cape where we lived, I was startled when I turned the corner into the living room to notice there was someone sleeping on our sofa bed. All I saw was dark hair and a body twisted in a blanket. I thought it was my mom. Suddenly, this body started moving, unraveled itself from the sheets, and sat up, revealing my Aunt Rita.

I was puzzled. Why was Aunt Rita here? Maybe she had presents for me. She was always going through her things and giving her old jewelry and trinkets to me and my cousin Robin. Was that why she was here? Where was Mommy? Seeing my confusion, Aunt Rita happily announced that mom was at the hospital and I now had a little sister named Teresa.

A sister. I had a sister. I was immediately concerned about how this new arrival was going to impact my life. Mom said if she had a baby girl that I would have to share my room with her. But I didn't want to share my room. I loved my room. It was my magical place where classrooms and playhouses were created. It's where I starred in the plays I made up in my head. It's where I dressed up in my mom's old gowns and costume jewelry and pretended I was a queen from a faraway land or a nightclub singer. My room was the most special place in the world to me, and I didn't want to share it with my new sister. Besides, she was bald! I couldn't even play hairdresser with her.

But I did get to play babysitter, which provided me with a sense of authority I eagerly accepted. Mom used to put Teresa in a white plastic car seat propped up by two large L-shaped metal legs—quite a flimsy thing compared to today's bulky contraptions—while I sat on the floor next to baby Teresa. "Just keep her entertained while I cook dinner," mom often said.

I wasn't really sure how to entertain a baby. But I sure tried my best. I talked to her. I sang to her. I danced for her. But Teresa just screamed, a piercing scream that hurt my six-year-old ears. This was not fun. I wanted to go back upstairs to my room where there was an imaginary classroom waiting for me. "Mommy, why does she scream like that?" I asked, practically screaming myself. My mother answered very calmly, "Well, Ann Marie, she's frustrated because she can't talk yet, and she has a lot to say."

Like most things, Mom was right about that.

**

I remember going to the pediatrician's office once. Teresa had come down with a cough or something. She was a little older than two, I was about seven, and my brother Patrick was a year older than me. Mom packed the three of us into our 1966 dark blue Ford Galaxy for a visit to Dr. Silberberg.

Like most kids, we hated going to the doctor. It seemed no matter how they tried to fool you with baskets of toys and pictures of Disney characters on the wall, there was always the fear that a needle was in your future. To help allay those concerns, Dr. Silberberg had a nurse on staff who spoke to the toddlers and preschoolers in a saccharine voice to cajole the children into thinking they were all there to have a good time. But Teresa saw right through that charade.

When we arrived at the doctor's office, the three of us were immediately lured in by the puzzles and toys tucked in the corner of the waiting room under a giant picture of Dumbo. After playing beneath the strong fluorescent lights for quite some time, my mother's name was called.

My mother tried to pull Teresa away from the wooden blocks she'd been playing with, but Teresa planted herself firmly and started to make a fuss. As if on cue, a saccharin-sweet nurse skipped over to make small talk with this defiant toddler. "And how are youuuuu today, Teresa?" My sister looked at her, annoyed, and snapped, "I'm sick. Why do you think I'm here?" Patrick and I roar with laughter. My mother was mortified, "Teresa!" Although terribly embarrassed, my mother couldn't help but laugh when we shared the story later with our relatives.

You never knew what Teresa was going to say. Her feisty personality belied her tiny body and angelic face. I think that's when my mother first said what she continued to say for years to come, either with embarrassment or awe depending on the situation, "That Teresa! She's something else."

We all knew early on that *that* Teresa really was something else.
But it was more than her quick wit and fervor that shocked and delighted us.

***

A strange thing happened one day in 1972. We were in the tiny bathroom of our small Cape. I was sitting on the edge of the bathtub facing Teresa, who was on the potty, as she called it.
I'm not sure how the conversation began, but Teresa said things to me that I couldn't understand. Most of which I was never able to recall. It was as if she was in a trance as she spoke very matter-of-factly about

God. Things that would happen in the future. Information that was far beyond the intellect or imaginings of a three-and-a-half-year-old girl. The one thing I do remember her saying, and it was that memory that brought it all back years later in a flash, was, "Ann, don't you understand? I can even remember being in Mommy's womb." It struck me later how odd it was that she used the word *womb* at that age and not *belly*.

This was the first of many metaphysical conversations Teresa and I had throughout our lives. It's a reference point in my mind when I think of my sister and how she seemed to know things, how she fearlessly went through life like a steam engine, as if she were invincible and at the same time as if she needed to go fast because there wasn't enough time for her to do everything she wanted to do. In a sense she seemed reckless to me. She did things I was too afraid to do, and I don't know why that is. We were raised with the same fears from our well-meaning family, religion, culture, and society. But Teresa? She didn't let anything get in her way.

That Teresa! She was something else!

Chapter 4

Sisters Alike

Teresa and I were always very close, and I don't say this lightly. We were and are closer than any two sisters I have ever known fictionally or in reality. I always felt like when I was talking to her, I was talking to myself—someone who understood me inside and out.

When I introduced Teresa to my friends, it was as if they already knew her because I referred to her in conversations even when she wasn't with me. We didn't look alike, but we had almost the same mannerisms and voice, only hers was a step higher.

It was our energy, mostly, our presence—only Teresa was more intense. I often told people that my sister was just like me, only to the eighth power. Their mouths would usually open wide and slowly let out, "Oh. My. Goddddd."

Like Teresa, I've never been afraid to speak up. Not in a mean way or without filters. Well, perhaps when I was younger. I do recall being told that I could be "a bit caustic at times" during a performance review when I was twenty-four. But I'm fueled by a sense of empathy and justice. I'm usually the only person in the room who says what needs to be said or does what needs to be done. I've always been that way.

As a kid, I would be the one to invite a newcomer at school to sit at my lunch table and introduce them to my friends. I could never understand why nobody else thought of inviting them. And if someone was being bullied, I would defend them at any cost.

Not long ago I was at a wake with my eighty-two-year-old mother where we were made to wait outside in the one hundred-degree heat to limit the number of people in the funeral home. Meanwhile, guests were "illegally" sneaking in through the exit door whenever someone left the building, further extending our sweltering wait. Everybody in line saw what was happening. But I was the one who walked up to the front of the line and opened the door to a grumpy old funeral usher and insisted he put someone on patrol at the exit door. The people waiting in line applauded me. My mom chuckled, half proud and half embarrassed, "That's my Annie taking charge."

But not everyone saw my actions the way Mom did. Throughout my career in corporate America, I was often called out as difficult. I was told my passion for great work was read by others as aggressive. I conducted myself no differently than any man around the conference table. But they weren't told they were difficult. No. They were challenging others to think. They were being assertive, "leaning in," and taking the lead. It didn't matter if I offered a better solution to a design or a headline. Like the time I questioned a project owner for wanting me to create a promotional calendar without our company name or logo on it. True story.

Teresa faced the same destiny in her field of medicine and in her charity work. Granted, she might have been a bit more abrasive, like to the eighth power, but she didn't back down. She often called me crying and screaming if she butted heads with someone in medical school or when she was working at the hospital.

So when she questioned an attending physician about treatment or suggested a different diagnosis, she was reprimanded. And, of course, no one offered an apology when it turned out this young doctor was right after all.

Censorship was a reoccurring theme for both of us. But we refused to dim our lights to make other people feel comfortable.

Chapter 5

Calling All Angels

Teresa was the only one who really believed me when I first started talking to angels. Friends might have thought my experiences were interesting, but while they wouldn't come out and say it, I knew they didn't fully embrace them. Teresa and I were equally electric. It was this aspect of our relationship that truly bonded us.

We grew up Catholic and went to church every Sunday at any cost. I loved St. Augustine's, a tiny old church that smelled like frankincense and had angels painted on the ceilings. As their luminous faces looked down on me, I imagined myself flying with them. After mass, I went into my parents' bedroom and somehow hefted the huge Bible my mother kept on her dresser onto her bed. Beautiful illustrations of angels appeared on almost every page.

Over time, my fascination with angels faded along with the rest of my childhood fantasies. I no longer imagined angels hovering around me offering their protection. Other than admiring masterful paintings in museums and art books, I didn't pay much attention to them.

But in the mid-to-late 1990s angels made a huge comeback. Suddenly, angels were everywhere. It seemed every day that I encountered an angel: either pinned on someone's lapel or hung around their neck. Gift boutiques and card stores with signs and tchotchkes proclaimed, "I Believe in Angels." It became kind of a craze, and I thought it was weird.

But all of that was about to change.

In the winter of 1998, after working full-time for almost twenty years, earning my bachelor's degree in the evenings, performing regularly at a local New Haven theatre, and rehearsing my musical project, I quit my job and became a stay-at-home mom. I decided to hell with everyone who insisted my family couldn't survive on only one income. Motherhood was priceless.

I reconnected with the simple joys of life. I lived at a slower pace and had more time for creativity and imagination. The disconnect from the negativity and stress of the outside world changed my energy. I was in a positive and loving place.

That's when I first started talking to angels.

And before long, I was talking to dead people, too.

Chapter 6

Lois

My sixteen-month-old son, Micky, looked like a chubby little cherub with his long auburn curls, large dark eyes, and striking features. One day, he decided that the family room needed some rearranging. He had pretty much knocked over every item within his grasp, but he felt more finishing touches were required.

Against one wall, I had a small wooden bookshelf that housed all of my Signet Greek tragedies and Shakespearean masterpieces from college. The shelves were deep, allowing for two rows of books on each shelf. It had been so long since I had a chance to sit and read that I didn't even remember half the books that were there anymore. Perhaps my son sensed this as he proceeded to stick his little hands between the books and clear them off the shelves, revealing rows of books I hadn't seen in years.

Later that evening, after I finally got my little interior decorator to sleep, I began to clean up his creative mess. As I approached the huge pile of books lying in front of the shelf, one caught my eye. It had a picture of an angel and was entitled *Angels Among Us*. I picked it up and flirted with the idea of forfeiting my much-needed sleep and treating myself to a book. Maybe I could get through a chapter or two before Mick got up.[1]

---

[1] I've searched for the author of this book, but cannot find it. I did find a book that appears to be the book I am referring to, but the copyright dates do not line up.

I settled in on the couch and was quickly intrigued as the author, whose first name was Trudy, told an incredible story of how she got the name of her guardian angel. I wanted to read on but knew I was on borrowed time. I headed for bed to catch an hour of sleep before Micky would wake.

After I settled into bed, I decided to try to find out who my guardian angel was. "Okay," I said to myself, "I would like to know the name of my guardian angel." It was strange how quickly it happened. In my mind, as if looking at a blackboard, gray letters spelled out Lois. I just laughed and said, "Alright, Lois. If you're my guardian angel, please let me know."

During this period of my life, I began to notice that my innermost thoughts and prayers were reflected back to me throughout the day. It might be the lyrics from a song on the radio, a newspaper headline, or a license plate on a car ahead of me. Sometimes it would be overhearing two people talking next to me while waiting in a checkout line. It felt like guidance, that I was on the right path. I started to call this phenomenon "getting confirmation." I decided to take this same approach with Lois and waited for her to confirm her name.

A week later, on Christmas day, I was standing at my stove stirring up the best pot of Italian sauce, filled with meatballs, sausage, and braciola. My mother arrived just in time to help me with the final preparations. Obviously, my sleep deprivation had led to insanity because I had offered to host the holiday festivities at my house. But with the help of my wonderfully organized Sicilian mother, everything was under control.

While we were scurrying around the kitchen, my mother was unusually talkative, telling me about a woman she wanted me to meet. I half listened as I busied myself between the dining room and kitchen. Sensing my inattentiveness, she grew slightly agitated and more excited as she listed all the things this woman and I had in common. The more she talked, the more animated she grew.

It was uncharacteristic for my mother to get excited in this way, especially when there was a task at hand. Finally, I stopped what I was doing and looked at her, "Fine, Mom, what's her name? I'll call her."

"Her name is Lois!" my mother beamed.

Chapter 7

No Coincidences

My mother believed what happened with Lois and me was due to some mystical gift I possessed. I never saw it that way, not even back when it first happened. I knew the name Lois magically appeared in my mind, and my mother's uncharacteristic enthusiasm that I meet a woman of the same name was a message for me. Skeptics in my circle of friends downgraded what I believed to be a mystical experience to a coincidence.

I don't believe in coincidences.

I believe in timeless interconnectedness with all that is.

Like when you suddenly start thinking of someone you haven't seen in twenty years and they call you. Or you bump into them at a supermarket that you hadn't even intended on going to.

Or one morning you realize that it would have been your grandmother's one hundredth birthday, had she not passed the year before. Then five minutes later you get a call from your sister-in-law, who never calls you. In fact, you don't even like each other. But she is desperate for an address she believes you have. And you happen to remember that address is written on an envelope from a card that you kept in a box in the back of your closet that you haven't opened in years. As soon as you open the box, there is a picture of your dead grandmother staring you in the face.

Yeah. Like that.

Whenever I need reassurance, I ask Lois to give me a sign.

Aboard a boat in the Caribbean, I asked Lois to give me a sign that every-thing was okay and looked up to see a nearby boat anchored with the name "Lois" painted in large letters along the side.

At an airport, I was struggling in my relationship with Petr when a random woman introduced her daughter to me as Annie Lois.
When I was on the phone with an ER nurse who prayed with me as my brother-in-law fought for his life, before we hung up, she told me her name was Lois.

At my father's bedside in intensive care after triple bypass surgery, nurse Lois assured me everything would be okay.

When you stop calling them coincidences and acknowledge something is happening beyond this physical world, you allow your experiences to expand. That's what happened to me. Lois had knocked on my door, and I decided to let her in.

And then shit got real.

Chapter 8

Yellow

I woke up with a decision that I was struggling with. So I made a leap and asked Lois for help. If the answer to my question was yes, I asked that she would somehow communicate the color yellow to me. And if it was no, she would do the same with green. I set out my intentions and then went about my day.

When lunchtime arrived at work I decided not to go out, something I rarely ever did at this particular job because I was experiencing severe censorship and bullying. But for whatever reason, I ate my lunch at my desk that day.

Since I worked in Cubicle Land, I could hear everything going on around me. Lunchtime was particularly quiet, though, because most had gone out and the phones tended to ease up then. After a short while the receptionist's voice broke through the silence in the cubicle behind me, "Bob, I have someone on the line for you from a company called the Yellow Company? I've never heard of them. Do you know who they are?" Bob said he had never heard of the Yellow Company.

The call wasn't for Bob. It was for me.

I'd figured out a way for Lois and me to talk to each other.

So I kept talking to her.

Next, it was the color purple. I asked Lois to communicate the color purple to me to give me reassurance about my marriage. Among the tulips that bordered the large porch of my Victorian house, where no purple tulip bulb had ever been planted or bloomed, appeared a purple one smack in the middle.

A few months later, I began to doubt Lois's reassurance of my marriage. So I asked her again. Later that day I was flipping through an envelope of photos from my cousin's wedding. There was a great photo of Petr and me that I wanted to frame. I had seen the photo several times, but this time I noticed something in the photo I had never seen before.

A single purple tulip tilted in a bud vase near my left arm.

Next, it was the number two. I asked Lois to show me the number two if the answer to a question I had was yes. Immediately after posing my question, two pennies dropped before my feet after I pulled my hands out of my pockets. Even I was skeptical on that one. So I asked Lois for a redo. Five seconds later, I was staring at two more pennies above my kitchen sink. I liked her style. Not only the number two again, but two pennies as if to make her point crystal clear.

"Are you writing this shit down?" Teresa's enthusiasm and excitement had waned, and now she started in on me. I had called her, still clutching the two pennies in my hand. "Yes!" I wrote every experience down in my journal. I eagerly awaited her praise. "What? So you can reread it ten years from now? You need to write a book." This is where we get to that eighth power thing. Teresa was always thinking big. I think list, she thinks book. I wavered. "I don't know if I'm ready to write a book yet."

Excuses didn't exist in Teresa's world. If she saw a potential for manifestation, she acted upon it. And she expected the same from me.

She pushed me forward when I didn't believe in myself. "I don't have enough experiences for a book."

Another excuse.

"So go get more!" I could hear her clattering cans and crackling cellophane as she optimized her pantry. She was always doing three things at once, and naturally expected the same from me. "Why don't you sign up to teach one of those continuing education classes at one of the high schools? Share your experiences and then give them an assignment to find out who their guardian angel is!"

My sister was brilliant.

I offered two sessions on two consecutive Thursdays. The class actually sold out to about twenty-five students. At the end of the first class, I asked the students to go through the same process I did. They were to ask for the name of their guardian angel and then ask for confirmation.

And it worked.

The following Thursday, the class was electric. Students were wiggling in their seats with excitement as they waited to share their experiences. Judy was the first student to share. She told the class the name Penny immediately came to her. The next morning, she went to make her coffee and realized she had forgotten to stop at the supermarket the day before to grab some. As she headed out to her favorite coffee shop, a thought popped in her head to go to a different coffee shop. When she walked up to the counter, she was greeted by a smiling woman wearing a name tag. Her name was Penny.

Other students shared very similar stores. As we approached the end of class, a woman who hadn't said much in either class shyly raised her hand. "It happened to me too," she said. She told the class about her penchant for reading. She took ten to fifteen books out at a time and stacked them in a basket near her reading chair. Once she started a book, she explained, she was insistent that she had to finish it before she would allow herself to start another book. Even if she didn't like the book she was reading, she felt obligated to plug away until the end.

She told the class she had gotten the name Nora and then asked for confirmation. The next evening after dinner, she sat in her chair and picked up a book she had been reading. She didn't really like the book, and for the very first time put it down and grabbed the next book in the pile.

It was dedicated to Nora.

Chapter 9

Sausage and Peppers

I decided to give my mom the same assignment I had given the class. She protested somewhat. "Mom," I said, "do you mean to tell me that you believe God created Eve from Adam's rib and parted the Red Sea, but you can't make this leap?"

My mother is a devout Roman Catholic. She goes to church every Sunday without fail, prays to the Infant of Prague, and says her Rosary daily. In fact, just the other day when I called her, she didn't pick up, but she did text me back.

"I can't talk now. I'm saying my Rosary."

Hmm...

Despite her faith and devotion, Mom had never shared any type of mystical experience with me, or any of us kids, for that matter. I might go as far as to say that Mom was a skeptic, not in God, but in herself, and in her ability to experience the mystical.

The next morning, she called me, "Alright, Ann Marie. I did what you asked me." "That's great, Mom. What name did you get?" Long pause. "Jezebel!" she said, somewhat confused. "Why does that name sound familiar? Isn't there a story about her in the Bible?" she continued.

"Yes, Mom!"

"Well, how come I don't know it?" she demanded. No question where Teresa got her feistiness from.

"Because you're Catholic, Mom, and Catholics don't read the Bible," I jibed.

Mom laughed, but continued, "Well, who was she?"

"She was a prostitute, Mom."

She shrieked. "What?" Now why in the hell would I get the name of a prostitute?" she demanded through shock and laughter.

"I guess God has a sense of humor, Mom, and apparently wants to get your attention."

The following morning, Mom called again. She told me that after we hung up the day before, she went grocery shopping and suddenly had a craving for sausage and peppers. She picked up the ingredients and decided to make it for dinner. When she got home, she realized she had forgotten how to make it and started to go through her cookbooks. Seriously, Mom, you're 100 percent Italian and you don't know how to make sausage and peppers?

Mom's church, a Roman Catholic church with a very large Italian population, had put together a cookbook of their parishioners' favorite Italian recipes. Naturally, Mom thought there would be a fabulous sausage and peppers recipe, and she eventually found it. But before she did, she randomly opened the book to another recipe.

It was a recipe for Jezebel Sauce.

She screeched, "Can you believe that?" And then she continued to repeat the story several times as if she was trying to convince herself that this had really happened.

I couldn't wait to tell Teresa. Like me, she found our mother's introduction to her angel, Jezebel, humorously appropriate. Teresa laughed, "It figures Mom would get confirmation about her guardian angel in a catholic cookbook naming a biblical whore."

Meanwhile, Teresa was still waiting to get confirmation of her guardian angel. She called me one day, forgoing any salutation or pleasantry, and said, "She's not giving me confirmation!" A few days earlier, Teresa stayed awake long enough to get the name Vera. "That's okay. Just ask her again," I offered gently, hoping to calm her down a bit. "I did! I followed the same process. Just like you told me. And it's been three days, and I still haven't gotten confirmation." As if her angel's lack of follow-through was somehow my fault.

I wondered if Vera was trying to teach Teresa something about patience, but I decided not to share that with my sister.

The next day I was having lunch with one of my colleagues, who was also a friend. Jen shared my mystical enthusiasm and was eager to hear about my angelic experiences. Finally, I told her about Teresa's frustration with Vera. "Only my sister could be annoyed by her guardian angel." Jen began to laugh and then stopped when something caught her eye. She pointed at the wall behind me. I twisted my neck to follow her finger and saw a four-foot, wooden capital letter *V*. Why it was there or what it stood for, I had no idea. It wasn't even the first letter of the name of the restaurant.

It was the first letter of Vera's name.

Teresa was thrilled to hear about my verification of Vera but frustrated with her inability to make the connection on her own. She understood why it wasn't happening—immediately. We both did. Teresa's life was chaos. She had just enough energy to get through the day. Aside from her medical practice and a new baby, she had gone back to school to get her master's degree in metabolic medicine. She just couldn't keep still long enough to notice anything around her.

So Vera found me in a restaurant instead.

Chapter 10

Angels Among Us

My mystical encounters with angels were a focal point in my life. And even though Teresa did not have first-hand experience, she was with me on that journey in a way that no one else was. A few years after Lois entered my life, something truly marvelous happened. As with Lois, it happened on Christmas.

It was close to midnight when I had gone to bed. After turning out the lights and relaxing, I felt my body gently start to vibrate. And then I began to rise what seemed to be about a foot above my body. Going out of my body was not a new experience for me. But what happened next was.

Almost immediately, a magnificent golden light enfolded me. It was a luminous, almost blinding light. Then, in an instant, my entire being was engulfed with a feeling of love so intense, like nothing that I had ever felt in my life. It was overwhelming. I could actually feel the vibrations from it pulsating throughout my body.

After what seemed like only a few moments in this state, I began hearing the most beautiful music. It was the strangest thing. I had never heard this music before, yet it sounded so familiar. It was as if there was a two hundred-piece orchestra of violins, harps, chimes and other instrumentals I had never heard before. It was utter bliss.

I believed I was in the presence of the Divine.

The experience seemed to go on all night. When I awoke the next morning, everything was fresh in my mind, as if I had only left it a moment before. I was still lying on my back, the same position I had been in when I went to bed. I rolled over to my left side to face my husband Petr. I couldn't wait to tell him, but he was still sleeping. So I just lay there staring at the back of his head and his beautiful long blonde hair. As if feeling my eyes boring into him, he turned around quickly, opened his blue eyes widely, and in his Czech accent, asked, "Baby, you were turning on lights last night? I thought it was the middle of day."

What was this? I thought I had drifted off to another place, but I guess I hadn't. This presence came to me. In my room. It was a visitation of the most beautiful and profound proportions. I had no words. There were no words. But within my Being, I felt a sense of peace unlike anything I had ever felt in my life.

I couldn't wait to call Teresa. I knew better than to call too early. Even a visit from God would not give me a free pass to impose on her precious sleep. No one dared to call Teresa early in the morning, except my father, Jack, of course. He would call her at 6:30 a.m. to wish her a happy birthday. And rather than be happy that our often aloof and forgetful father had remembered her birthday, Teresa would scold him, "Dad, how many times do I have to tell you not to call me at six thirty in the morning?" She would literally scream at him. So, what did Jack do? Call her a week later at 6:30 a.m. when he was putting the turkey in the oven to wish her a happy Thanksgiving. Why? Because nobody yelled at Jack.

I waited until ten o'clock to call Teresa. She answered the phone with a sleepy, "Oh my God. I've got a serious sugar and gluten hangover. Did you survive Christmas? How was . . ."

Before she could finish her sentence, I excitedly began, "You're not going believe what happened to me last night. I mean, you probably will, because you get it, but this was so incredible . . ." I started going off on a tangent, and she cut me off: "Just tell me what happened already, will you? " Patience was not one of her virtues, but when I began to tell her what happened, she fell silent.

When I was finished, she said, slowly and in the quietest, gentlest voice just above a whisper, "What the hell?" And in the next second, she boomed, "When are you going to stop dicking around and write that book?"

Did she really have to be so crass at a moment like this?

She went on like that for a while. She was "Tottenizing" me, a word we derived from our maiden name, Tottenham. We coined it because whenever we needed to hear some truth from our dad, or even unsolicited but valuable advice from one of his seven siblings, they did it with a certain style. They were thoughtful but tough. Fiercely loving but righteous.

They lit a fire under our ass.

I was being *Tottenized* by my sister. And I absolutely adored her for it!

As I look back at it all now, Teresa's scoldings had a sense of urgency. She wanted me to get on with it. Had she known something I didn't know?

Chapter 11

Ann Marie Loves Herself

When I was ten years old and Teresa almost five, my mother and new stepfather purchased a huge two-family Victorian house. We had outgrown our little Cape with the arrival of our brother Frankie in 1972, and two years later we were moving. Teresa and I were excited about the move. The house had two bathrooms, and our new bedroom had a double window that looked out to trees instead of the street,

My stepfather, Frank, tried so hard to be a good father and husband, but he suffered horribly with bipolar disorder and severe mood swings. His fits of mania and depression disrupted our family life throughout my childhood. For some reason Teresa and I received the worst of it.

After about twelve years of marriage, his bipolar episodes ceased, and he entered a state of depression that never subsided. And at the age of thirty-nine, he took his own life. Sadly, at that time, he and I were not on speaking terms, which is something that I have regretted for many years.

Twenty years later, my mother remarried and moved out of the house to live with her new husband, Tom. Now divorced, I jumped on the opportunity to live in the amazing home I grew up in. I felt this would provide Mick with continuity, having spent a lot of time there with me. It wasn't ideal, but it was the next best thing. I had mixed feelings, too, wondering if I could live in a house that held so many painful memories with my stepfather. Unfortunately, I didn't have much choice. The price was right. The space was huge. And I knew the landlord.

I had been living in my childhood home for over a year. How I loved that old Victorian house! I was enjoying a cup of freshly ground, perked coffee. "What a glorious feeling," I thought to myself. Mick was with his dad, and I had the entire day to do whatever I wanted. While I had long ago unsubscribed to the notion that Saturday was "cleaning day," I was somehow feeling that was just what I wanted to do.

I sipped my coffee and made a game plan in my mind. Even though virtually every room needed attention in this huge old house, I decided I would focus on the kitchen. I smiled as I imagined how clean and beautiful my kitchen would look and smell by the time I had finished giving it a good cleaning.

During this period, I had been working on positive affirmations as instructed in a book that I was reading. That day's lesson had been learning to love yourself. I glanced at myself in the mirror and said, "I love you, Annie!" With a wink and laugh at my reflection, I headed toward the laundry room to grab my cleaning supplies and prepare to work my magic in the kitchen. As I stepped out of the laundry room to enter the kitchen, I stopped, turned around, and took a good look at the laundry room, which was by far the ugliest room in the house. The brown contact-papered cabinets that hung above the ancient washer and dryer were peeling and loaded with boxes, vases, and memorabilia that I'd inherited from my mother when I had moved in. The floors were classic '70s red brick linoleum. If that wasn't enough, the plaster walls had holes in them, which caused bits of white specs to constantly fall over the floor.

With complete disregard for my previous plan to clean the kitchen, I suddenly found myself tearing through the cabinets and drawers. After about an hour, I realized that I was not going to leave that room until every cabinet had been purged of junk and every corner dusted, vacuumed, and washed. I also realized that I was not going to achieve my original goal of cleaning my kitchen, which was in dire need of my attention. "Oh well," I thought. "I guess this is where I'm supposed to be today, so just go with it," and, oh yeah, "I love you, Annie!"

After several hours of cleaning, sorting, and proclaiming my love for myself, I was finally done. Exhausted, I grabbed some homemade iced tea from the fridge. With a deep sigh and sense of satisfaction, I stood in the doorway admiring my magnificent work. I couldn't believe what a difference I had made in this little space. I had taken down a set of curtains that had probably been hanging for over twenty-five years. (Okay, Mom, I'm sure you washed them at least once.) Now, more light was visible in the room. As I glanced over the doorway which led into the garage, something caught my eye. The removal of the curtains revealed a large section of wall above the doorway. I could see brush strokes in the shape of letters that were hidden under a layer of paint. It looked like a sentence. I tilted my head to avoid the reflection from the overhead fluorescent lights so I could make out what was written. Finally, I could read what it said.

"Ann Marie loves herself."

I had completely forgotten.

Many years ago, my stepfather, Frank, painted the very laundry room I was now standing in. Frank suffered from bipolar disorder, which made life very difficult for all of us. You never knew which Frank you were going to get: "Funny Frank" or "Angry Frank."

What seemed to trigger Frank most was that he lacked what I had in abundance: confidence. And when Frank was on the war path, he told me that I was stuck up and found reasons to ground me. He always apologized after these horrible episodes. But this was the pattern I learned to live with.

One day, after a two-week "dark phase," he sat me down at the kitchen table and took the time to explain to me where he believed all of his anger came from and told me about his abusive father. I felt so bad for Frank. He was such a beautiful man, but his father had absolutely ruined him. And when he got in his dark phase, I reminded him of all the things he was not. He told me that my self-confidence was a good thing and that he was sorry for making me feel bad about it.
And then he got changed into his painting clothes.

After priming the walls in bright white paint, Frank decided to play a joke on me and wrote "Ann Marie loves herself" in very thick brown paint. Later, he used the paint roller to go over it, but the thick brush strokes still showed through.

I thought about the two students in my class, each getting confirmation of their angels' names in the context of doing something they'd never done before. Mom getting a sudden and overwhelming urge for sausage and peppers. Me, hell-bent with visions of a sparkling, clean kitchen, and instead ripping down a pair of curtains to reveal my daily affirmation painted on the wall. Were the angels and dead people planting thoughts in our minds?

Was the source of inspiration actually Divine influence?

Chapter 12

Jimmy Miller

Jimmy Miller was handsome, highly intelligent, and brilliantly funny. While our meeting and courtship were magical, we were both so young. Jim and I divorced after only a few years of marriage. Sadly, twenty years later, he was killed in a tragic car accident.

Jim and I did not have a friendly parting. He was an unforgiving Scorpio, and that was the end of it. I was estranged from his family after the divorce but felt like I had to reach out to his mother after he died. I wrote her a letter eulogizing Jim and expressing my deepest condolences for the loss of her youngest child.

Jim's mother received my letter with gratitude. She wrote me back, accepting my request to pay her a visit. It was strange being back at the house where our courtship had begun, the memories thick. I was overcome with regret and sadness, but I knew I had to be strong for Jim's mother. I kept myself collected, and we had a nice visit.

After the visit, I got in my car and said aloud, "Jim, I know you were there today." With 100 percent faith he would hear me, I turned on the radio, knowing he would play a song confirming my statement to him.

And he did.

A neighbor of Jim's once shared a story that always stayed with me. The neighbor, about eight years older than Jim, said he would never forget the time when Jim's mom was driving with Jim and this neighbor in the car. This neighbor told me, "The song 'Wooly Bully' came on. And there was little Jimmy in the back seat, who could barely talk, but knew all the worlds to 'Wooly Bully' and proceeded to sing it."

Not surprisingly, "Wooly Bully" was the song blasting through my car speakers on that day as I left his mother's house.

That's how it works.

A couple of years later I was presented with another opportunity to reach out to Jim. This experience was one of the most incredible, and it was the third to happen at Christmastime.

It was time to put up the Christmas tree, and I was particularly grateful for the help from my cherub. Mick, who was now sixteen, could haul a tree from atop my car, drag it through the house (of course spraying needles everywhere), and put it in the stand.

After getting the lights on the tree, I decided to take a much-deserved break. I sat down on the sofa, took a sip of water and placed my glass on a Christmas coaster that was now part of my holiday decor. I chuckled, remembering that I had received the coaster set from Jimmy's family on our first Christmas. Out loud, I said, "Remember this, Jim? A Christmas present from cousin Bill, circa 1987." I sipped my water and wondered if he would let me know he heard me, especially since he had done so in the past. I decided to send a telepathic intention to him, asking him to give me a sign that he heard me make the remark about the coasters.

Then, for no reason, I turned on the TV and clicked on a movie. I didn't know why I did that. I had only planned on taking a short break and certainly didn't have time to watch a movie.

But before the night was over, I found out why.

The movie I selected looked like it could be an interesting romantic drama, and I thought maybe I would watch it another time. I had to get back to the tree.

I don't believe I've ever decorated a Christmas tree without listening to Andy Williams's Christmas album. But since the passing of my father, I knew the music would make me sad instead of getting me in the Christmas spirit. To keep things festive, but light, I asked Mick to find a silly Christmas movie for us.

Mick popped in the movie Elf with Will Ferrell in the DVD player, and I knew immediately his laughter would be better than any nostalgic Christmas music.

My decorating strategy was to work at the back of the tree first. Then, by the time the opening credits were done, move to the front of the tree where I could see the TV and enjoy bits of the movie while decorating.

I worked furiously, grabbing ornaments from the coffee table and quickly scooting behind the tree to hang them, frantically scattering ornaments and not paying too much attention to how they looked. Who was going to look in the corner at the back of the Christmas tree anyway? Oh right, my mother.

Now I was ready to move to the front of the tree. As I grabbed an ornament off the table, I turned to look at my giant TV for the first time since the DVD started. I stopped dead in my tracks. I couldn't believe what I saw on the screen.

In the largest typeface imaginable, in bold, capital letters and less than two feet from my face, was my ex-husband's first and last name glowing in high definition.

JIMMY MILLER.

(My ex-husband and the executive producer shared the same name.)

I froze for a second, gasped, and then started crying. It was that powerful.

Mick came around to see what happened, and I told him through my tears. "Mom, this stuff happens to you all the time. Why are you freaking out like this?" I collected myself and told him it was because it happened only minutes after I asked Jim for a sign. And it wasn't just any sign. It was his name! No it was his full name! Not a song that reminds me of him. Not a popular expression we both used, or any other way he could have let me know that he heard me. He literally got in my face.

And the moment I made that connection, I knew intuitively he must have done that for a reason.

Of course, I immediately called Teresa and told her what happened. She was blown away but then quickly frustrated, "Dill, how do you do this shit?"

Okay. I need to take a moment to explain our pet name.

Teresa and I had coined the name Dill for each other years before when she had flown home during a break in medical school to help me with Mick after he was born. How did such a pet name come about? Well, let's just say that in a moment of exhaustion and frustration, Teresa was ranting and raving about someone who had gotten on her last nerve. I was continually amazed at my sister's ability to string together a great number of trashy words so quickly in such moments, but this particular evening in the Big Y parking lot was by far one of her most prolific moments. I can no longer recall exactly what she said, only that in this classic, all-star delivery of Teresa trash talk, the word Dildo was used in a way that no one on earth would ever think to use it. I laughed so hard that I literally (and when I say literally, I mean it) was on the ground. Teresa was laughing just has hard and would have joined me on the ground had she not been holding three-month-old Mick in her arms.

Thus, our pet name "Dill" was born, a code word that brought about thunderous laughter at any given moment, and later an endearing pet name for each other. Of course my clever sister quickly expanded upon "Dill," creating usage in virtually every part of speech.

Now I felt bad teasing Teresa with this incredible experience with my ex-husband and leaving her hanging. "Sorry, honey. I don't have time for a Dill session right now. I just had to tell you what happened. I'll call you later so we can talk more about it." Then I went back to the tree.

At some point Mick had departed to his room and left me with the final touches. Now I was finished and packing up the ornament boxes. As I sat on the sofa putting the last bits of tissue paper in the boxes, I thought about Jim the entire time.

"What did you want to tell me, Jim?" I said aloud to the quiet room set aglow with Christmas tree lights.

I stacked the boxes near the attic door and sat on the couch to call Teresa. She answered the phone immediately, "Hey, Dill, you doin' alright?" I answered her with a question. "Do you understand how amazing this is?" She asked, "Dill, what the hell, man?" We often talked like this, throwing questions back and forth at each other. "I just know he wanted to tell me something."

The moment the words left my mouth I knew what it was.

The movie!

The movie that I had briefly watched popped into my mind, and the answer came spontaneously and quickly. "Oh my God! Dill, I know what he wants to tell me! The scene I watched portrayed a man telling his wife that divorcing her was the biggest mistake he ever made in his life. (And an interesting twist in the scene was that the man didn't realize his ex-wife was actually dead and he was talking to a ghost.)

Thats's why Jim so earnestly wanted to get my attention. He wanted to apologize to me.

The very moment I understood his message, my hand fumbled upon a ball of tissue paper that hadn't made it back into the box when I was cleaning up. I squeezed the paper gently and realized there was an ornament in it.

I unwrapped the tissue to find a tiny glass, red heart that Jim gave me on our first Christmas in 1986. I knew instantly this was Jim's way of telling me that I had indeed understood his message loud and clear.

Teresa, still on the phone, listened without interrupting as I connected the movie to Jim's message. Finally, she broke the silence.

"Dill, you need to teach me how to do this shit."

In less than four years Teresa began to have the most extraordinary mystical experiences. The only difference was that she was the dead person sending messages from the other side

Chapter 13

Going Down

Despite my dead stepfather reminding me that I loved myself, angelic beings visiting me in my bedroom, and my dead ex-husband popping up on my TV screen, I got little traction on the book Teresa continuously nagged me to write. For a few months I was enthusiastic and committed, writing every day, and then, as I always seemed to do, I gave up.

I blamed my lack of commitment and follow-through on two things: a lifelong struggle with procrastination and the melancholy that leveled me each February. As far back as I can remember, February has always been a tough month for me. And the procrastination and abandonment of my goals seemed only to fuel my February blues. But the truth was that I hated myself for not finishing my book, for not living up to my potential.

As I got older, the February blues became even more intense. I was unrecognizable to my friends and family. I struggled to keep up a pretense of my former self in front of my colleagues. If it wasn't for Teresa, I don't know how I would have gotten through any of it. She was the only person I really cared to talk to. She understood what I was feeling because she, too, had experienced her share of depression and antidepressants. Although it played out differently for her.

Since she was a doctor, it required little effort on my part to get a prescription for an antidepressant. All I had to do was ask her. I tried to hold off as long as I could, hoping and praying that I would wake up and feel like myself again, but I usually started the pills in March. When summer came along and I started to feel like myself again, I would start to ween myself off them and be finished with the drug by August.

And that became my cycle with antidepressants.

For a while anyway.

Chapter 14

My Sister's Place

In September 2014, Petr and I booked a trip to see his parents in the Czech Republic. The day before we left, I had planned to go to the bank during my lunch hour to exchange some currency. Since the bank was literally down the hill from my house, it made sense for me to work from home after I finished my banking.

At twelve thirty, I grabbed my many bags from my cube, said goodbye to my workmates, and made my way to the on-site gym for a quick workout before heading out to the bank.

Like most people, I listen to music when I work out. Generally, I select the shuffle option from my massive collection of music, jump on one of the cardio machines, and hit the play button. On that day, the first song that came on was "Aquarius" from the musical *Hair*. The song hadn't come up on my playlist in a very long time. In fact, I'd forgotten it was even in my library. Talk about a song to get me moving. I felt imbibed with so much energy. And to my surprise, I became covered with chills and started to cry. It wasn't a sad cry, more of a cry of joy.

The song is about the Age of Aquarius, a time that I knew was almost upon us. The lyrics describe a future where the planets would arrange in a way to create very specific energy to help end falsehoods and derisions and create harmony and understanding on earth. For some reason these lyrics struck me in a very powerful way.

The chills would not subside, nor would the tears. People were now looking at me, somewhat concerned. But I just smiled through the tears. When the song ended, I wanted to hear it again. So I selected the repeat option, listened to the song over and over again for my entire forty-minute workout, and continued to listen to it while I changed in the locker room.

I got in my car to head to the bank and checked my watch. It was 1:10. Okay, I thought, fifteen minutes to get to the bank and then two minutes to get home from there. I started my car, and as if I hadn't already heard it enough, I wanted to continue to listen to "Aquarius." I had an old phone that didn't have a Bluetooth option, so I just listened through my phone as it lay on the passenger's seat next to me.

Now with time alone, and away from the stares of the people at the gym, I felt a knowing within me that this song was hitting me like this for a reason. There was a connection between the lyrics, my chills and tears, and my incessant desire to hear it over and over again. I came to a stop light, paused the music, and put out an intention to the Universe. I didn't know if I was addressing God or Lois, but out loud in my car, I looked up and said, "I feel so strongly that you're trying to get my attention with this song. Like it's a message for me? If I am right, please can you give me confirmation?" I said thank you, resumed the music, and continued singing, "Let the sunshine, Let the sunshine in . . ."

About thirty seconds later, with the bank only a couple of turns away, I ran through my to-dos in my mind: "Okay, after I log off from work, I'll make my checklist, start packing, leave house instructions for Mick . . . *go to my My Sister's Place.*" At first, I didn't realize that this last suggestion did not come from me, but without thinking, I answered it absently in my head, "I don't have time to go to My Sister's Place and try on clothes. I have to get to the bank and get to my two o'clock meeting." Immediately, the voice answered, "*Just go in the back and look at shoes.*"

In the next instant, without even thinking about it, instead of heading straight to where the bank was, I found myself taking a sudden right turn and pulling into the back parking lot of My Sister's Place. As suggested by the voice in my head, I walked into the store through the back entrance and then took a right where the shoe display was. My Sister's Place was one of my favorite thrift shops, and I often scored some really great pieces there. But today I was standing in front of the shoes as directed by the voice in my head.

Tempted by a few styles, I slipped off my heels and started trying on shoes. It's amazing how quickly a display of well-priced designer footwear can make you forget that you need to be in two places within fifteen minutes. I guess that's why I didn't hear it at first—the soft, mysterious-sounding flutes and piccolos trilling up the scale in a curious arrangement. It was the steady, familiar percussive rhythm that got my attention, "Dum dadum dum, dum dadum dum . . ." I jerked my head up from the row of shoes that I was browsing and looked around to see where the music was coming from. Hanging from the ceiling, above the shoe display, was a pair of old dusty stereo speakers. I stared at the archaic blocks of wood in absolute awe and disbelief as "Aquarius" began playing softly overhead.

The familiar chills vibrated all over my body, and I nearly fell to my knees. What on earth was happening here? How did God or the Universe or whatever it was just orchestrate this seemingly impossible scenario? I was so attached to very specific tasks, which were likewise attached to an inflexible timetable, and a voice in my head told me to go shoe shopping? And—as if waiting for me to get into place—right on cue, the same song that I had been listening to repeatedly for the last eighty minutes begins to play. I continued to stare at the speakers, the chills intensifying throughout my body. It hadn't even been ten minutes since I had asked for confirmation, and now here it was. But what was the message? Why was this song playing for me?

I needed to talk to Teresa. I reached for my phone to call her and saw that it was almost two o'clock, *"Shit! I'm going to be late for my meeting, and I definitely won't make it to the bank."* I bolted out of the store and jumped in my car. It was only two minutes to my house, and I would have just enough time to log onto my work computer and only be a couple of minutes late for meeting.

At 3:05, I dialed my sister, hoping that since she didn't see patients on Friday, she would have time to talk to me. She answered on the first ring, "What's up, Dill? Getting ready to fly to Europe?" And without even answering, I launched into the incredible experience that happened in My Sister's Place.

"Oh my God, Dill," she said. "I'm completely covered in chills." And I guess for that reason she didn't launch into her typical tirade about me writing my book. She listened attentively as I regaled her with the extraordinary events that had taken place. "This is blowing my mind on so many levels, Dill," I said to her in almost a whisper. "I asked a question to the Universe and was answered immediately. Not the next day, or the next week, but in five minutes." That in itself was incredible and fantastical. But what resonated deeply for both of us about the experience was that it felt like a call to action—to what neither of us knew. What we both seemed to intuitively understand was that whatever I needed to do would be revealed in Divine timing. The whole experience was simply epic.

(I struggled while writing this last sentence. I couldn't decide if epic was the right word here. I kept typing it and deleted it. It seemed like the perfect word, but I wondered if it sounded too dramatic. I decided to go with it. I typed the sentence, "It felt epic," and then

glanced at my phone to see the time was 11:11 a.m. It was the right word. You'll see what I mean soon enough. Read on.)

Chapter 15

In the Flow

It had only been a few weeks since God told me to go to "My Sister's Place" and then cued up "Aquarius" for me. I hadn't yet figured out what that glorious moment meant, but I continued to bask in the joyful afterglow from the experience, which attracted more wonderful synchronicities. Everything in my life unfolded organically and beautifully, providing me with what I needed precisely when I needed it.

I was challenged and well paid in a new job that I loved and had been in for over three years. Every project assigned to me went smoothly. My husband and I were in sync and entering into a wonderful period during our relationship. My son was graduating from high school. And I was singing in an incredibly tight blues rock band with one of my best friends, Zito. At the top of the list, I got to see Teresa a lot. I remember she figured out that between 2012 and 2014 we had seen each other eleven times, a number that would soon have great significance for both of us.

For some reason, the Aquarius experience affected Teresa too. It was as if it had linked us both up to a higher vibration that attracted the right people and timely opportunities to move us toward our purpose.

One Saturday evening, I got a call from Teresa. "Hey, honey, what's . . ." I started, but she cut me off. "Oh my God, Dill, I just talked to Caroline Myss!"

Teresa —competing with thousands of listeners worldwide—was able to speak to Dr. Caroline Myss during a live radio broadcast that both of us listened to regularly. Dr. Caroline Myss is a five-time *New York Times* bestselling author and internationally renowned speaker in the fields of human consciousness, spirituality and mysticism, health, energy medicine, and the science of medical intuition. During this time, Teresa and I were probably on our fifth book by Caroline, each one bringing us a greater understanding of our spiritual nature and connection with the Divine.

"Can you believe I got through? What are the chances, right? Anyway, I told her that I was an MD transitioning to energy medicine and wanted to know which of her upcoming conferences would be the most helpful for me. Caroline told me that I should go to the one where Dr. C. Norman Shealy would be with her. Dr. Shealy was a neurosurgeon and pioneer of holistic medicine who worked with Caroline when she first stepped into her gifts as a medical intuitive. No wonder Caroline suggested that conference. Teresa and Norm had a lot in common.

Teresa made such an impression on Dr. Shealy that he invited her to Missouri to be his guest at his weeklong certification class for energy healing.

Teresa's chance meeting with these two extraordinary people was instrumental in her transition to energy medicine and created a lot of excitement for her. We called and texted each other multiple times daily.

It was right around this time that Teresa began to see the number 11 everywhere. She noticed she would catch 11:11 a.m. and p.m. daily, and 11 after the hour constantly. If she placed an order, got a dry cleaning ticket, or was staring at a license plate in front of her, there would be 11s. She was convinced these numbers were a message for her, and she was right.

Now, before you start saying I'm "cuckoo la-la," hear me out. Everything in the Universe has energy, including numbers. From sacred geometry to numerology, these are symbols with meaning. Shapes and numbers break language barriers between countries and Universes. Everything and anything can be reduced to a number, from the alphabet to our chemical makeup.

Just as with astrology, numerology is a very old and complicated science. It takes decades to understand numerology and more to become fluent enough to use it as a tool to understand your life path and how the numbers you carry in your birth, name, and more affect your life.

The number 11 is a master number representing intuition and enlightenment. When you repeatedly see this number, it means that you have understood, accepted, and believed a message—that you should trust that you're going in the right direction.

With this phenomenon happening immediately after the mystical "Aquarius" experience, and her timely education with Caroline and Norm, we both felt like we were being led to our purpose.

And we were right.

(I just finished writing this section and said out loud to my sister, "What an amazing period of our life that was, Dill! So much was happening back then when you were the human named Teresa." Ready to take a break, and always checking the clock right before I do, I stared at the time. It was 11:19. Teresa's birthday. And an 11 too. I know she is here with me writing this book.)

Chapter 16

Right Place. Right Time.

I had only been back from the Czech Republic for a couple of days and was at work fighting through the lingering jet lag. I was happy as 5:00 p.m. neared. And wanting to get home to my sofa even quicker, I decided to leave ten minutes early so I could get ahead of the rush of people heading for the elevators, and the traffic.

I quickly got in and out of two elevators to make my journey to my car, only to realize that I'd left my cell phone back in my office. There was a time when such an inconvenience and loss of time would infuriate me. But after hearing "Aquarius" at My Sister's Place, I had learned to trust that wherever I was, was where I was supposed to be. I was actually smiling and humming as I repeated my journey in reverse, back to the two elevators.

The halls were now busy with people making their way to various stairs and elevators. When I got to the second elevator, I had to wait a couple of minutes for it to arrive. Glancing around and humming as I waited, I browsed a bulletin board behind me that was covered with flyers for apartments, festivals, and a variety of offerings. My eye went to a flyer that was offering tickets for a speaking engagement featuring Elizabeth Gilbert, author of *Eat, Pray, Love*, a book that Teresa and I were very intrigued by, as Elizabeth's experiences of Divine synchronicities mirrored what we were both currently experiencing. I didn't know how much the tickets were, if they'd all been sold already, or if both of us would be free on the date of the show.

I just knew we were supposed to be there.

I quickly ripped off the paper tab with the phone number. I couldn't call Teresa yet because I knew she was still seeing patients, so I texted her, "We're going to see Elizabeth Gilbert." Teresa called back almost immediately. "Hey, what's going on?" she said when I answered the phone. I told her how I was in the right place at the right time when I saw the notice on the bulletin board. The logistics were going to be a bear for Teresa since she would have to go directly to Newark from Dr. Norm Shealy's in Missouri. But, like me, she knew we were supposed to see Elizabeth Gilbert together. "Hurry up and call before someone else gets those tickets," she insisted. "Dill, relax," I said. "Those tickets are ours. I promise you." And they were.

We cleared our calendars for the weekend of September 26, 2014.

Our weekend in Newark was the most mystically charged weekend of our lives.

Chapter 17

Newark, New Jersey

Teresa arrived at the hotel in Newark before me and was impatiently waiting for me to get there. I had texted her before I left Connecticut to tell her that there were bomb-sniffing dogs at the Amtrak terminal in New Haven. That made her nervous, and she told me I should skip the train and just drive. But when I told her I felt good about it in my gut, she uncharacteristically acquiesced, and I won the battle. By then, both of us were learning to trust our guts. But when I arrived in Newark, there was another situation, and I was yet again delayed. Apparently, there was some terrorist alert and they were stopping trams to hotel transport.

I called Teresa to tell her what was going on. That was it. "Alright this is bullshit!" she exploded. "You need to get the fuck out of that terminal now. I'm calling a car for you." I just laughed because—I have to admit— it was beyond entertaining when Teresa was all fired up about something. She was always hitting the panic button. "Dill, relax," I said. "I'm calm and not concerned about this at all. Trust me, okay? I'll be there soon." "Alright," she finally resigned softly. And then, agitated and loudly, "But don't dick around and grab a coffee and do all your stupid shit. Come straight to the hotel. I ordered room service, and I'm sitting here staring at it waiting for you to get your sorry ass here." Yes. This is *exactly* how she talked. And for those of you on audio, that was exactly how she sounded.

After bomb-sniffing dogs, train delays, and a halted hotel shuttle from Amtrak to the Hilton, I texted Teresa to tell her that I was heading up to the room. When I got off the elevator to our floor, she was already there, strutting her power walk with her hands in the air, screaming, "Woohoo! Dill! We're together again!" We practically threw ourselves at each other, embracing tightly, rocking left to right, and then quickly pulled apart.

We had this thing about hugging each other.

We always fiercely hugged hello and just as intensely goodbye. But that was the end of it. We never hugged each other at any other time. No hugs good night or good morning. We would give everyone in the family a Merry Christmas hug, and then we would look at each other and throw our hands up as if to say, "Yeah, we're good." This was so very strange because we were huggers. We hugged everybody, even strangers. I adored my sister more than anyone, yet I felt really weird hugging her.

I finally asked her about it one morning when we were having coffee in her living room. "Tre, I gotta ask you something. Is it just me, or do you not liking hugging me either?" She had almost spit out her coffee. "Oh my God!" she began. "I can't stand hugging you. I mean, I'm good when I first see you after a long time and when we have to say goodbye, but other than that, I am not comfortable hugging you at all."

So she felt the same way. "Dill, what do you think that's about?" I asked. She thought for a second and said, "I don't know. I think maybe I let you down in a past life and there is a lingering dissension there." It sounded plausible, but who knew, neither of us ever having done a past life regression. But I was just glad I had finally brought it up, and not really surprised to learn that she had felt the same way.

Now, after hugging in the middle of the hotel hallway, Teresa grabbed my suitcase and started marching down the hall in a fabulous fitted sweater dress and four-inch heels. She looked beautiful, thin, and fit with her signature calf muscles accenting her magnificent legs. She was nearly to the room when she turned around and yelled, "And get this! My flight got in at 11:11."

I had to laugh when I walked into the room. Teresa had cleared the clock and phone off one of the nightstands and loaded it up with her Xymogen supplements and shakes, mini shakers of Himalayan salt, gluten-free bread and snacks, non-dairy butter, avocados, a can of garbanzo beans, and more. All of these were staples in our lives that my sister never traveled without. Mind you, we were staying at a Hilton with a fabulous restaurant, but Teresa always traveled like this. I wouldn't have been surprised to see her toaster oven, which she often carted along on road trips, lest she be forced to use a microwave. I benefited from Teresa's expanded knowledge of nutritional and anti-aging medicine. Thanks to her, both of us had redefined our bodies and were living our healthiest lives, feeling and looking pretty fantastic.

As we dug in to the healthy and delicious lunch Teresa had ordered, we were electric. We couldn't contain our excitement about the serendipity that had brought us together.

But it was so much bigger than that. The number 11 seemed to appear everywhere, underscoring and validating conversations and moments of knowing. It was as if we were being told, "Yes. You're correct. Continue in that direction."

There was magic in the air.

Chapter 18

Total Recall

Hearing Elizabeth Gilbert recount her incredible journey of synchronistic experiences that led her from despair to joy was the ultimate confirmation that Teresa and I were also being led deliberately in the direction of our destiny. We kept nudging each other with a look that said, "You believe this shit?" Elizabeth completely validated everything I had been experiencing and what Teresa had just begun experiencing. She was speaking our language, and it infused us with electricity and inspiration to continue to pursue our passions.

I felt inspired to create a vocation based on the experiences I was having. I didn't know what, but I was thinking that I could help people tap into their spiritual nature. Meanwhile, Teresa, already armed with education and experience and on the heels of a massive dose of education and inspiration from Dr. Myss and Dr. Shealy, was ready to turn her medical practice inside out.

Our last night in Newark, September 28, 2014, was the pinnacle of the weekend. We didn't think we could get any higher.

But we did.

(As I sit here writing this section, I suddenly realized that today is September 28th. The same date that years ago Teresa and I had our mystical revelation! After I made that connection, I wrote, "Our last night in Newark . . ." and my phone dinged with a new text. I picked

up my phone to see that it was currently 11:11 a.m. I knew that ding was Teresa confirming the connection I'd just made. And to make doubly sure I knew, the text was a screenshot photo from my friend Abigail showing the timestamp 11:11.)

At the end of the event, we grabbed dinner at the hotel restaurant and continued to see 11s on our watches, phones, restaurant bills, you name it. Since it was our last night together, we wanted to make the most of every second. We both had an early start the next morning, so we packed up most of our belongings so we would have time to relax and talk.

Lately it had seemed that all of our conversations had the same theme. We both felt that our collective synchronicities were happening for a reason. "What does it all mean?" we pondered in between pulling our clothes off hangers and putting them in our suitcases.

Teresa sat on the bed and started twirling her hair. I saw the familiar faraway look on her face. She was about to figure it out. Still staring off, she said, "Everything that's been going on with us, the reoccurring numbers, the time we've been able to spend together, you hearing 'Age of Aquarius' in that store. It all means something. I know it."

I sat down next to her. "What do you think it is, Dill?" I asked softly. And before she could answer me, and as if answering my question, a long-forgotten memory popped to the forefront of my mind, like total recall, "Wait!" I think you do know why all of this is happening." Confused, she asked, "I do?" "Yes." I said. "I think you told me when you were little. I completely forgot about it until this moment."

Divine timing strikes once again, I thought.

"What are you talking about? What did you completely block out?" she was growing impatient.

I told her what happened that day in 1972 when we were both in the bathroom. "What? How come you never told me this?" she asked. "Honestly, I only remembered it right now. You were saying all kinds of things that you couldn't possibly have known, and you were scaring me. One thing I feel very strongly is that whatever you were talking about had to do with the two of us."

Flashes of the conversation were coming back to me. "I just remembered something else," I said. "I'm pretty sure you said something to me about your death." Maybe that's why I was so scared. "My death? What did I say?" But I couldn't remember. "I don't know. I can't recall the details, but in this moment, I have a faint memory of you talking about things that would happen in the future and saying something like, "I even know when I'm going to die." "Wait a minute, I said that?" she asked wide-eyed. "Tre, that's all I remember."

We sat in silence for a couple of minutes.

"Did I ever tell you about the dream I had about the end of the world?" Teresa asked. "It was the most vivid dream, like a lucid dream. You and I were sitting in a car somewhere together, and Frankie (our brother) was driving. I think it was in front of the Holy Rosary Church. As far as we could see, everything was on fire. It was apocalyptic, Ann. And then all of a sudden Jesus was walking toward us, and I turned to look at you and said, 'See. I told you he was real!' and then I was wide awake."

"Tre, are you kidding me? I had a similar dream when I was nineteen! When you said the word *apocalyptic*, the memory came to me immediately. Only, in my dream, there was flooding everywhere. I was paddling a boat to rescue people, and I couldn't fit them all in the boat. When I looked up, I saw Jesus walking on the water toward me."

"Holy shit!" we said practically in unison. She continued, "And you don't even connect with Jesus anymore. You're always talking about your angels and dead people. Why don't you ever reach out to Jesus?" She was getting worked up.

"I don't know. I guess my ego is in the way. I don't want to be associated with Christian extremists." Teresa listened intently, and then said, "I hear what you're saying, but don't throw the baby out with the bath water. I feel like he is somehow part of whatever it is we're trying to figure out," she said.

It was getting late, and we had an early start. We brushed our teeth and each got in our queen-sized beds. "This is just like the old days," I said. "Two beds with a night table between us." "I know," Teresa said. "It's perfect, Dill."

As exhausted as we were, we couldn't sleep. We were so charged up from our conversation and the events that had unfolded over the past few months. Finally, Teresa said in the darkness, "We have a mission, Ann. I'm not saying we're going to be rescuing people from fires and floods. But it feels like we're supposed to help people somehow. Maybe the dreams were a metaphor. I don't know." We lay in silence for a while. "Tre," I said sleepily. "Our Jesus dreams?" "Yeah?" she answered in a yawn. "I think they have something to do with the voice that told me to go to My Sister's Place and hear 'Aquarius.'" "Yeah. I definitely feel like it's all connected," she said in a yawn. "It feels like we're being pointed to our destiny, our mission. You know? The reason we decided to come here in the first place."

I knew she was right.

Chapter 19

All the World's a Stage

Reality is merely an illusion, albeit a persistent one.
—Albert Einstein

I've done a decent amount of research in the realm of spirituality, near-death experiences (NDEs), past-life regressions (PLRs), out-of-body experiences (OBEs), mediumship, you name it. Thousands of people having NDEs, PLRs and OBEs have reported similar experiences, themes, and understandings. I've also read the works of many brilliant, highly educated spiritual teachers who underscore the findings of these individuals through their own research, first-hand experiences, and study of ancient texts and archeology.

Before we incarnate here (or anywhere, for that matter), we are pure energy, spirit, a light fragment of God, the Universe, or Source Energy —whatever you wish to call the omnipresent, omnipotent force that gives us form. We are pure consciousness. In this state of pure consciousness, we have access to a higher level of understanding and knowing than what we possess as physical beings. For one thing, we get to know our soul family. These are the "people" we reincarnate with again and again. For example, your mother in this life might have been your daughter in a previous life. Your best friend might have been your wife or your husband. In this space, you remember everyone you've had a connection to and the various relationships you've had together.

If we choose to incarnate, we not only choose our purpose, but we also make agreements, or "sacred contracts," as Caroline Myss, PhD, calls them, with individuals in our soul family who will assist us in our mission, meeting our contractual obligations. And at the same time, we are likely assisting them in fulfilling their "sacred contracts."

Now this generally begs the question, "Why would anyone choose to be born with spina bifida or have a child who dies of cancer?" At the human level, we would never want to experience either of these scenarios. But as pure consciousness, we are not deterred from experiencing such travails and suffering that offer the opportunity to expand our consciousness to a level of even greater knowing. And on it goes until we no longer have the need to come here or anywhere else, for that matter, unless we want to.

In spirit or pure consciousness, we have a different vantage point, an awareness and knowing that we do not have in physical form, but we arrive here forgetting everything! Our goal as physical beings is to fulfill our sacred contract and remember that we are pure consciousness, a cell in the body of God.

Of course, the upside of being here is we get an incredible tactile and emotional experience that allows us to enjoy the deliciousness of being human. But the ego keeps us from our pure nature by wanting, desiring, and needing things: people, wealth, love, sex, food. When we over-focus on the enjoyment of these humanly pleasures, they become unhealthy attachments that weigh us down energetically and prevent us from remembering and awakening to our true nature.

I watched a very insightful interview with artist and author Natalie Sudman on Awake and Empowered TV. After her NDE, Natalie saw reality in a whole new way. She explained that we are like actors in a play, choosing the parts we will play. We might say to a member of our soul family, "Hey, how about we all get in a car crash, and I'll end up a paraplegic in a wheelchair and you have to take care of me for the rest of your life? Wouldn't that be cool?" We would never even imagine such aspirations in the human form, but again, as physical beings, we have a very limited perception of the whole and complexities of reality. The greater our challenges are in this physical life, the greater the spiritual growth.

Producer and director Darryl Anka uses a great analogy to give us a sense of what it might be like for us as pure consciousness to choose a particularly challenging life experience. He says it's like going to see a scary movie. You grab your friends and sit with your popcorn and candy watching horrors unfold. You are a voyeur getting the pants scared off you. But it's just a movie. And when it's over, you're fine. You leave and go home. And that's what we do when we're done here. We leave and we go "home" to our origins.

When we die, we leave our physical body and return to pure consciousness. Almost every single person who has had an NDE reports a nearly identical experience. They see brilliant white light and feel an intense and indescribable feeling of unconditional love. They recall being greeted by their loved ones and even their pets, which helps make the transition from the physical to the non-physical less shocking to our system. After this reunion, we experience our life review, which provides an opportunity for us to see all of the times we did not act out of love. It's been reported that this is a very painful experience at the soul level, however necessary for our spiritual evolution. At some point, we are guided toward our next experience, which could include returning to earth or an incarnation in another realm of reality.

There are thousands of recorded accounts of NDEs and probably hundreds of thousands more unreported. One that stands out among them is the experience Anita Moorjani wrote about in her book *Dying to Be Me*. Anita's family sat around her hospital bed, waiting for her to die. Weighing under ninety pounds, Anita was riddled with cancer, with over twenty lemon-sized tumors in her body. One by one, her organs began shutting down. Doctors told Anita's family that she was in the final stages and that it wouldn't be long now. What no one knew was that while they were waiting for her to die, Anita's consciousness, her Being, was far away in another realm. There, she understood how she ended up with cancer. Anita had spent her life suppressing her truth in order to please others and gain their approval, namely her father. Her unresolved and unreleased guilt, shame, and anger festered into cancer. When she understood this, she returned to her body and had a spontaneous healing, which could not be explained by her doctors.

Anita's extraordinary experience and that of other NDEs is a precious gift to humanity. Yet there are still people who aren't buying it. If they were to believe Anita's testimony, they would be forced to believe that they are responsible for creating the situations and relationships in which they now find themselves. Marianne Williamson said it best: "Our deepest fear is that we are powerful beyond measure."

We crave structure because it makes us feel safe. An experience like Anita's and thousands and thousands of others forces the scientific paradigm to come tumbling down like a game of Jenga, and the predictable structure of reality that has made us feel safe is pulled out like a rug from under our feet. Everything we believe to be true is called into question.

Change is scary. Better to dismiss it as cuckoo la-la.

Chapter 20

Sweet Surrender

Teresa and I talked until early in the morning and rose at 5:00 a.m. to make our departures. We hugged each other goodbye, a little misty-eyed. We were both tired, but the conversation from the night before left us both vibing high. As we pulled away from our embrace, we agreed we could keep following the signs that we were both sure would lead to our mission.

After Teresa left, I still had another ninety minutes to catch my shuttle to Penn Station. In the early morning quiet, I washed my face in silence, feeling calm and peaceful in a way I never had in my life. I was staring at my reflection in the mirror, searching my face, wondering what I was supposed to do next to help the mission unfold. And then I heard in my head, "Surrender." There's that word again, I thought.

Along my journey of spiritual awakening, *surrender* was a word that always came across my path. And it scared me. I was a bona fide type A personality. But if I wanted to know what my mission was, I was going to have to let go of egoistic attachments and control and surrender to my spiritual nature.

I stared at my reflection in the mirror and said, "Yep. It's time, Annie. Here goes: God, I know I'm a bit of a control freak," I began, "but I'm ready to let my Spirit take the wheel." I instantly felt light, really light, actually, and a little playful. "I'll even shave my head if you want me to, but, um, I hope you won't ask me to do that," I said, laughing.

And in the next breath, without even thinking about it, I started talking to my first spiritual teacher. "Jesus," I said, "I know it's been a long time since we've talked. I'm sorry. I'm here now though. Please give me the guidance and protection I need so that I can fully surrender." I was immediately at peace.

An hour later, I stepped into the back seat of a taxi and headed toward Penn Station. I had a feeling of lightness that I'd never experienced. I sat in the back seat of the cab with a big ole grin on my face, not stressing about missing my train or getting delayed or who I'd have to sit next to. I trusted that everything would work out the way it was supposed to and felt free of any burdens. For the first time in my life, I truly understood what it meant to be living in the moment. I held no impressions of the past or concerns for the future. I held no thoughts in my mind that could shape any expectation of what would or should happen in the next second, minute, or hour of my life.

I was completely present. Completely calm.

The taxi pulled along the sidewalk and dropped me off in front of the station. It was a very quiet Sunday morning as I walked through the doors and made my way through the lobby to the track listings. After I found my track number, I headed off to find a quiet seat so I could listen to *Energy Anatomy* by Caroline Myss on my phone. As I came around the corner, there was a small convenience store selling books and snacks. I had no intention of going in, as I already had some healthy snacks packed courtesy of Teresa and plenty to read. Besides, I thought, these places are so overpriced, and I'm not going to spend $50 on a book.

And then that thing happened again, the voice in my head. "Just go in. Maybe you'll find something on sale."

I smiled and thought, *Sure, okay*. I walked up to a small carousel of books, spun it once, twice, and bam! This little book *God's Promises for Every Day* appears. Thinking about the conversation I had just had back in the mirror at my hotel room, I figured I was supposed to buy this book. So I picked it up and turned it over, expecting to see a $50 price tag. But to my surprise, it was only $4.97. How could I not buy it? I found a quiet bench and sat glancing through my new little book.

(I hadn't looked at that little book since that day at Penn Station, and I couldn't tell you why. I didn't even know if I still had it or if I gave it away during the move. But as I was writing this, I was curious about where it could be. I turned around and looked at the tiny bookshelf behind the chair that I was sitting in—one of many places throughout this huge house where I display my books—and without even scrolling the shelves, I was staring right at the title on the spine God's Promises for Every Day. *So I picked it up and noticed that at the top, there was a small, white card sticking out. It was a mass card. I cannot believe what I read on this card only a second after recounting the discovery of my and Teresa's mission, "Teresa Tottenham Sievers and you who mourn have been enrolled in the Trinity Missions Mass Society." What? Teresa and I are enrolled in a Mission? You bet we are!)*

Back at Penn Station, it was time for me to head to track 1—of course it was track 1—where my train would soon be arriving to take me back to New Haven. I reached the top of the stairs and started looking for a place to sit when I noticed this beautiful old black man dressed in his Sunday best— suit, tie, hat, and all. He was pacing back and forth, closely parallel to track 1, where my train would arrive in just a few moments. In his hand, he was clutching a Bible, and I could hear him mumbling something. Soon, the mumbling grew louder, and eventually he started yelling.

"I banish you, Satan. You be gone, Satan. Be gone, Satan."

He kept repeating similar phrases, sounding like a Southern preacher. He continued for a bit and then, once again, returned to mumbling. And as before, he began getting louder and louder, only this time he changed his chant.

"There's only Jesus Christ! Jesus Christ! Jesus Christ! There's only Jesus Christ! Pray to Jesus Christ!"

I was so glued to this beautiful little man, who continued to repeat his pattern of banishing Satan and invoking Jesus.

I thought about the declarations I made in the mirror ninety minutes earlier at the hotel. Hadn't I just asked for Jesus's love and protection?

This was weird.

I looked around, expecting to see people gathered around to watch this man. I was ready to make a stand against anyone who might jeer at him. But no one was looking at him. I scanned the crowd of people scattered on the platform, thinking I would surely see someone nudging a friend and tilting their head toward the man. But no one was looking at him.

No one seemed to notice him, or even see him.

Except me.

A sudden knowing came to me.

This little black man was a messenger sent to let me know my prayer was heard. And literally the second that thought popped into my mind, I looked up and caught a sign across the track. I had never seen a sign like this anywhere in all my travels through airports and train stations, and I never have since. There was no company name or logo, just a massive black poster with white knockout type that read,

"WHAT HAPPENS NEXT CHANGES EVERYTHING."

I froze. That message was for me too. I felt like I was being called out, as if the Universe was testing me, "Are you sure you are ready to surrender?"

I looked up at the sky and projected my thoughts back at the Universe: "Bring it on!"

Chapter 21

Joyful

If I had to put together a soundtrack to underscore the utter bliss I felt when I stepped onto the train that headed back home to New Haven, it would be without question the finale from Beethoven's Symphony #9 "Ode to Joy."

I called Teresa as soon as I got in my car to tell her what happened after she left the hotel. I started with the promises I made to myself in front of the mirror and ended with the Southern-preacher-looking guy at the train station and the gigantic sign with the strange message. Naturally, she freaked out and said the only thing anyone could say after an experience like that.

"Holy shit!"

My thoughts exactly.

We were both electric. We had no idea what to expect, but there was one thing we were both certain about: our work and our passion shared a common thread—energy.

Through our work we wanted people to understand that we are all energy connected to and affected by the energy within us and around us. We hoped to inspire people to re-examine their belief system and reconsider the magnitude of reality. For me it was connecting with departed loved ones, guides, and angels, something I hoped would help people heal their hearts. And for Teresa it was to use her expanded knowledge as an MD, powerful presence, and reputation to help people make the connection between their emotions and their well-being.

The epic message of Aquarius and our seemingly fantastical experiences in Newark sparked our spirits.

We were ready to take flight.

Chapter 22

Take a Chance on Me

My declaration of surrender planted an unshakeable peace deep within me. I embodied joy, and that vibrational frequency launched me into a fantastic creative period over the following five months. Conversations and situations seemed to show up at the perfect moment. Everything flowed without resistance. I was gliding down a stream, never worrying about getting caught in a current or smashing into a rock.

I danced through life.

I went back to my book again. I wanted to capture every mystical moment that happened over the last month and get serious about teaching people how they could connect with their angels and departed loved ones. I knew I was supposed to follow this inspiration. I thought about the students who shared their amazing connections with their angels in the adult education class I had taught years earlier. Ideas began to formulate in my mind. If a person could be a life coach, I thought, why couldn't I be a soul coach? The idea came to me so easily.

And a couple of weeks later I had my first client.

I had just wrapped up work on a very successful companywide marketing event, a tremendous professional commitment that requir-ed extra work and travel. But it also gave me exposure to many influential, high-ranking executives to whom I typically would not have access. The majority of them were directors, vice presidents, and chief officers—strong, confident, and intelligent women. I loved working with them. These women respected my intelligence and were not threatened by my passion and vibrance. It was an incredible team.

A group of us was finishing putting computers back in our roller bags and waiting for the corporate photographer to take a picture of our enormous team responsible for this event. One of the executives, Rachel, had complimented me on a stone I was wearing, which ultimately led to her telling the rest of us in the group a story about a stone she had recently purchased because, strangely, she had explained, she felt drawn to the stone and compelled to have it. I told her people are often guided to the right stone at the right time in the same way we are drawn into circumstances and people. I shared a couple of my own profound mystical experiences, never imagining I would be having this type of conversation with the head of our ethics department.

Yet the words just came out of my mouth so easily.

By now other executives were gathering around listening, very intrigued and interested in my experiences. Finally, Rachel said to me, "Annie, do you remember Raj, who chaired last year's Marketing Expo?" I told her I did. "Did you know she left the company and started her own marketing and branding company to help launch people who do the kind of work you are talking about?" I felt a pang of jealousy and a jolt of excitement at the same time. I couldn't believe what she had just told me. This was the most unlikely place for this type of information to unfold.

I knew this was validation for my soul coaching idea.

Boldly, in front of all of these powerhouse women, I announced, "I guess I should call her because that's what I'm about to do," and proceeded to explain that I was going to open a soul coaching practice." I completely surprised myself. Did I really just tell these executives that I was leaving my job and opening a soul coaching practice? I didn't have the finances in place or client base yet.

Then, to my utter surprise, Alice, my department's chief marketing officer, jumped in enthusiastically and beamed, "Well I want to be your first client."

Alice was going to be my first client? This was incredible! I looked up to Alice. Her story was inspirational. I knew where she came from and how she had worked hard and fought her way to the top in a man's world. There would be no half-assing it with Alice. I was going to have to have my shit together in a big way. And I knew that's why she was my first client. This was serious. Alice was a high-powered executive and didn't have time to play games.

I was going to have to show up for real this time.

A tiny voice inside of me, my voice this time, was in the background screaming, *"Are you crazy, woman? You never finish anything you start!"*

I told the voice to shut up. And I surrendered.

Chapter 23

About to Reach the Masses

Teresa's dream of teaching people to heal their bodies was starting to get legs. She continued to speak at various venues and wrote for more magazines. She even landed an in-depth exposé in a local magazine, that featured a gorgeous picture of her on the cover.

I was in my studio and didn't have my phone with me. When I picked it up, there were five missed calls from Teresa and a string of texts.

"Dill, where the fuck are you?"

"I'm calling you."

"Could you answer your fucking phone."

"You're killing me!"

"Call me!"

That was Teresa, alright.

"There you are! Finally!" she bellowed when I finally called her back. "Why can't you keep your phone with you? What if I needed you?" I tried to answer her, but she cut me off. "Dill, I'm going to be on TV! Can you believe it?" Her excitement was palpable.

Through a series of synchronistic events, Teresa met a producer in Texas while working on an infomercial. The producer, Doug, told her that he'd never seen a doctor with so much personality. Most doctors were dry and boring on camera. But Teresa was captivating, brilliant, beautiful, funny, and engaging. Doug later told me that he loved Teresa immediately.

Through the course of shooting the infomercial, Doug learned a lot about Teresa. He was aligned with her convictions about energy medicine and her passion for empowering people with alternatives to prescription drugs.

As a Western-trained medical doctor, Teresa was in a unique position to promote alternative and energy healing. It made people who might have been uneasy about straying from traditional medicine feel safe. After all, if a medical doctor was endorsing it, then it must be safe. Doug envisioned Teresa hosting a series on DR TV, interviewing alternative doctors and energy practitioners.

Teresa was about to reach the masses.

Chapter 24

Going Down, Again

Our magical weekend in Newark set off a chain reaction of events that we knew was part of our mission. And we surrendered to all of it. I had never felt so joyful and creative in my life.

And then February rolled around. Like clockwork, my depression kicked in.

I was getting ready for a band gig in New Haven. Zito and I had just hired two brothers who were phenomenal musicians on bass and drums. And our set list was killer. That's when I first noticed that something felt off. I just couldn't seem to get my mojo on for the performance. I looked at myself in the mirror. My signature '70s lace top. My brown leather vest and my bell bottoms. The hairdresser had just left. My makeup was flawless. And for no plausible reason, I felt the way I felt whenever it started—the depression.

I remember thinking, "Oh no. Please. I can't go back there." Everything in my life was so great, but it didn't matter. A force that I couldn't explain was pulling me down. By the end of that month, I felt even worse.

My wonderful new client wanted to meet with me, but I wasn't able to, and that made me feel even worse. I kept canceling our appointments. I stopped writing.

My inspiration and excitement were replaced with anxiety and melancholy. It was horrible.

I came home from work, plopped myself on the couch, and numbed myself with mindless movies. The weekend came, and I didn't care. There was no excitement. I had no interest in inviting friends over for my weekly "Saturday night dance party." I hated what my sadness was doing to my family. Like me, they couldn't understand how or why my joy plummeted. Seeing them worry about me only made me feel worse.

It was time to call Teresa and ask her to write me a script for an antidepressant.

"You know you don't need antidepressants," she said. I was surprised at her reluctance, and I could tell that she was irritated. "What you need," she began to explain, "is to get to the root of the problem and figure out *why* you get depressed every February."

"Mom gets depressed every February. I must have inherited that from her." And that's when she first mentioned epigenetics to me. "You're depression has little to do with genetics and everything to do with your emotions." I wasn't in the mood for one of her lectures. "My emotions? What are you talking about? Everything in my life is great. In fact, it's never been better! There is no logical reason I should feel this way!" I started to cry again.

She backed off quickly and changed from irritation to empathy. "Listen, honey," she said so softly and lovingly, "just because you can't access the emotions that are causing your depression doesn't mean they aren't the cause. And anyway, there isn't any conclusive data to support that antidepressants relieve depression." "Then how come they seem to help me?" I asked, confused. "They work because you believe they will."

She started to talk about some study. I don't know if it was blind or double blind, and honestly, I can't remember the scientific parameter. However, the aim of the study was to prove the placebo effect. The study had to do with a number of people who needed knee replacement surgery. In this study, all participants were treated in accordance with an identical pre-surgery protocol. All were put under anesthesia and awoke in the recovery room with the same post surgical stitches in their legs. All of them went through the same post-op treatment and physical therapy and recovered without complications.

But not all of them had the surgery.

I had to admit that I was fascinated by the experiment, but her attempt to dissuade me from pharmaceutical drugs backfired. "Good," I said. "Then call me in Wellbutrin. I believe they are going to work." She started to protest, again, and I cut her off, "Why are you giving me such a hard time? You've been taking Wellbutrin for years." I thought for sure I had her with that one. But she surprised me.

"I'm done with pharmaceuticals, Dill."

"What? How?"

"What do you mean how? This is what I've been studying for the past six years and busting my ass trying to teach my patients. And some of them don't want to hear it. I just tell them, 'Hey, if all you want to do is sit back and take a pill, then I'm not the right doctor for you.' You know— you write my articles for me."

Of course I knew, but I also knew that when it came to depression, neither of us wanted to take any chances. "So how are you dealing with your depression?"

Teresa shared the techniques she learned when she became certified in energy medicine a few months earlier with Dr. Norm Shealy. She spoke with such excitement and conviction as she explained the benefits of *biogenics brain training*, which uses a sound treatment and brain wave synchronization to induce the same mental state associated with meditation practice, only quicker. "You can find it online, but I'll send you the link. Just listen to it at night before you go to bed."

Teresa also used transcutaneous acupuncture, developed by Dr. Shealy. His signature Bliss oils—air, earth, fire, crystal, and water—addressed a range of physical and mental conditions, and diseases, including depression. Each morning Teresa applied the oils to specific acupressure points on her body.

She also talked about another energy healing technique in the realm of Emotional Freedom Techniques or EFTs, called *Tapping*, a powerful healing tool she believed would help me release the emotions that were at the root of my depression and causing it to show up every year.

This was the first I had heard about these new energy therapies and Teresa's new lifestyle. Lately, she had become so busy giving talks and traveling to film her television series, it was impossible for me to keep up with everything she was learning. Yet despite the lack of data for antidepressants, Teresa's personal testimonials, and the unwavering trust I had in her, I wanted the easy way out. I wanted to take a pill and be done with it.

As disappointed as Teresa was with my unwillingness to put the smallest amount of effort into my healing, she met me where I was. And like a good sister-doctor, she called in a prescription for the antidepressant.

In the meantime, I was in survival mode until the drugs kicked in. I didn't come back to life until May.

By that time, I had lost my client.

Chapter 25

Divorce is on the Table

I wished I had Teresa's fortitude.

While I was in Connecticut waiting for my antidepressants to kick in, Teresa took action. She was focused and determined to restructure her medical practice into a twenty-first-century wellness center that included Reiki, transcutaneous acupuncture, and Emotional Freedom Techniques and was always learning more non-invasive but powerful treatments that addressed body, mind, and spirit. At that time, there weren't a lot of doctors doing that, least of all medical doctors.

She interviewed marketing firms, met with videographers, did more radio and television interviews, and gave educational talks anyplace that would have her. She even connected with a local investment firm, where together they offered health-and-wealth talks, which gave her access to a new audience.

I still have a file on my computer with the articles I wrote with her, and website copy for her new television show *Pathways 2 Healing*. This was her mission statement: to awaken people to energy medicine as essential to their well-being and teach them how to activate the body's innate ability to heal. It's hard to believe this statement came from a medical doctor board certified in internal medicine.

I envied Teresa's persistence. She was a multitasker of epic proportions. She could nurse her baby, study for a board exam, and curl her hair at the same time. And in the middle of all that, she could make an apple pie from scratch, feed the homeless, and help me figure out my life. She kicked ass in life like no one I have ever known.

She capitalized on the momentum from our weekend in Newark, work-ing harder, longer, and faster. That Teresa was going to reach the masses, and no one was going to get in her way.

Except her husband.

To this day, people ask me how someone as intelligent and intuitive as my sister ended up with Mark Sievers. There are a few reasons, actually.

From the beginning, Teresa was conflicted about Mark. There were qualities she loved about him, but unfortunately, his shortcomings would have driven a saint batshit crazy.

Teresa had only been divorced a short time when she met Mark, and her broken heart hadn't yet healed.

Mark was the perfect salve for Teresa. He showered her with attention and affection: love notes, flowers, little gifts just because, a never-ending stream of compliments and kisses, endless desire for her. What woman doesn't love that? For Teresa, it was like a drug that she needed badly, and she was pretty hooked on it.

But in so many other ways, they just didn't match up.

Teresa was more of a *Masterpiece Theatre* girl, a *Scrabble* girl. While Mark was interested in mens wrestling and comic books. For the most part, Teresa tolerated that. She compartmentalized.

Teresa was brilliant, driven, focused, and the life of the party.

Mark was scatterbrained, seemingly oblivious, and awkward. That's the bit that conflicted Teresa and later got under her skin. And that was the bit Mark used to fool us all.

It's not like Teresa didn't see his shortcomings before they were married, but they were manageable back then. Besides, Mark offered Teresa other perks that she simply could not resist, and I believe in her mind made up for his deficiencies.

Primarily, Teresa didn't like to be alone. She hated it. She was always afraid that someone was going to break into her house and attack her. Even when we lived together, she always heard noises. I'd go as far as to say that she was paranoid.

Teresa's new boyfriend, Mark, had a pistol permit and a collection of guns he wasn't afraid to use. And I think this made Teresa feel safe in a way she never had.

When you put it all together, Teresa had a guy who worshipped the ground she walked on and was her protector at all costs.

At least that's what she thought. It's what we all thought.

Mark made it a point to mitigate any and all stress in Teresa's life, giving her more time to focus on her practice and post-doctoral studies. If she needed something, Mark was there. The only problem was he would generally screw up the task at hand or forget to do it all together. "Forgetting" became Mark's excuse for everything. After they got married, this became increasingly problematic when he became Teresa's office manager and the kids came along.

Teresa did consider ending the relationship before marrying him. Deep down, she knew she didn't have the kind of love that warranted a marriage—the kind of love that made putting up with someone's bullshit tolerable. What she had was a personal assistant, albeit an incapable one, a bodyguard, and a man who made her feel like she was irresistible.

And the thought of starting all over again with someone else depressed her. She was in her thirties, and all her friends and siblings were married and having kids. Teresa wanted that too—the house, the picket fence, all of it.

Eventually, she came up with a solution for her conundrum with Mark Sievers. She called me up one day, "I figured out what to do about Mark." I listened intently as any good sister would. "I haven't been on birth control for a long time now, and I really want to have a baby. So if I get pregnant, then I'm going to take that as a sign that I'm supposed to be with Mark. Why not? Asking for signs is what we do, right?"

And one month later, she got pregnant.

Okay, wait. I already know what you're thinking. Why on earth would anyone choose this experience? Remember what I said about what you think is good for you and what your higher self thinks is good might not be the same thing? Well, there you have it.

Now, twelve years later, she was screaming and crying on the other end of the phone, "My fucking husband is making me crazy!" Those were the only words I could make out on that Sunday afternoon in January 2015. She alternated between screaming and sobbing. It was nothing new, actually.

I'd gotten many phone calls like this from my sister over the years. Mark wasn't the man Teresa thought he was. The man to take care of her. A partner in life who would support her so she could fulfill her goals and dreams. His once slightly annoying airhead antics now seemed purposeful and manipulative. His excuse for not picking up the kids on time, or making a deposit at the bank, or calling the insurance company, or a million other things was always the same, "I forgot."

The higher Teresa soared professionally and spiritually, the more Mark tripped her mid-stride. It was weird too. Like he would get off on watching her lose her shit, and lose her shit she did. The screaming matches were frequent and intense. We all wondered the same thing: *Is this guy for real? Did he just deliberately piss her off?* It kind of looked that way to everyone in Teresa's circle.

But Mark always knew how to get back on her good side.

He would say things like, "Mama, what can I do to make your day better? Would you like me to schedule a massage for you? Do you need me to go to the grocery store?" Every time he set her off, he found some way to remind her that he was her hero. That she needed him. Even if Teresa complained about something to Mark in passing, he stepped in and made a big deal about it, whether he was scolding a barista who gave her the wrong coffee or demanding a refund and a gift certificate if her massage or facial was subpar.

And if she heard a strange noise in the middle of the night, he was only too happy to pull his Magnum 47 from the night table drawer.

I had often suggested to Teresa that maybe it was time to end the marriage, but that was never an option for her. She said that her marriage to Mark was a sacred contract, not just in the context of the marriage covenant, but the sacred contract they both agreed to before they incarnated. I knew what she meant but thought that since she was on the brink of insanity, maybe she had already completed that contract.

But she wouldn't hear of it. "Divorce is off the table, Ann." Those were her exact words.

Now I was on the phone trying to make out what she was saying through her screaming and crying. I had never heard her like this. I could sense the hurt and betrayal through her tears as she sobbed from the deepest part of her soul.

What I finally learned was that Mark "forgot" to file the quarterly taxes for Teresa's practice. They were looking at a $30,000 tax bill.

"I am so over him, Ann! He makes me so crazy I could kill him."

Then she screamed an edict I thought I'd never hear from her, "Divorce is no longer off the table!"

Chapter 26

Red Flags

Mark gave me the creeps.

I was only in Mark Sievers' company two times before my sister married him. And it was the second time that I'll never forget. They weren't even engaged at this point.

It was the day before my dad's wedding in March 2003. Teresa and Mark had flown up to Connecticut and were staying at my house for the weekend. Teresa and I were so excited to be together and couldn't wait to party and dance together.

I had already met Mark a couple of times but couldn't get much of a read on him. There were always lots of family around. The only impression I walked away with was that he seemed to be overly affectionate with my sister and a bit goofy. Like he tried to be funny, but he wasn't.

I still hadn't settled on what to wear for Dad's big day the following afternoon, and I was running out of time. Teresa was outside with Mark. My brothers and the rest of my family were having drinks. I wanted her to help me figure out what dress to wear, and I wanted to get it over with so I could relax with everyone else. So Teresa told me to try on each dress and walk outside, and she would help me choose.

I headed to the guest bedroom at the back of the house where I kept my gowns and special dresses. I quickly took my clothes off, grabbed a dress, and threw it over my head. I slipped my feet into a pair of heels and walked through the house and out the kitchen door where everyone was. I looked at my sister and posed, turning around to model the dress. "Eh, it's alright. Let me see another one," she said.

I marched back into the house through the kitchen, dining room, and living room to the small bedroom. I quickly threw on another dress. I wanted to get this over with so I could hang out with everyone outside. I hurriedly charged out of the room and was startled to see Mark standing there in the living room. There was no reason for him to be in that part of the house. Everyone else was outside, and I barely knew him.

"You look really nice in that dress, Annie," he said just above a whisper. It was the creepiest voice imaginable. I felt completely grossed out, like I had just been violated. Not knowing what to say or do, I thanked him uneasily and continued walking quickly outside.

I avoided Mark as much as possible for the rest of the weekend, careful not to be alone with him. And I said nothing to Teresa. Despite the dark shadow he cast, the wedding was spectacular, and I enjoyed being with my sister and the rest of the family. But when Monday morning rolled around, I knew I had a decision to make, and unfortunately, Teresa wasn't going to be able to help me with this one.

I knew just who to call.

Daniele was a mutual friend of mine and Teresa's. They had been friends since high school, and I became very close with Daniele in 1990 when Teresa and I lived together. The three of us had a tight bond. Aside from being one of my closest friends and someone who could make me pee my pants from laughter, Daniele was brilliant, insightful, thoughtful, and decisive. I trusted her judgment, and she understood the unique closeness between Teresa and me. There was no one more qualified to help me figure out this dilemma. Only Daniele was equally stumped with what to do.

I didn't want to come between my sister and her husband. How could I tell her that I thought he was a creep? What if I was overreacting? Could I have been? Later I learned that most people in Teresa's circle felt the same way about Mark as I did. Even Teresa's male friends thought Mark was weird and inappropriate.

In the end, I decided to give Mark another chance. If he did anything remotely off-color, I was going to tell my sister to break up with that loser. Unfortunately, I never had the chance. Since they lived in Florida, there would be no Sunday dinners or family gatherings that presented an opportunity for Mark to reveal his true nature.

The next time I saw my sister's new boyfriend was at their wedding.

Chapter 27

What Happens Next Changes Everything

It was just a little after one o'clock on Monday, June 29. I was sitting in my cube pretending to work all morning, still tired from my mother's birthday weekend with my family in New York. I had some huge projects coming my way, including a newly assigned role as the content chairperson for our next annual marketing event. It was a load of work and a load of BS, and it could wait. I needed to recalibrate. I hadn't slept very well. My nieces and nephews woke most of the house at 4:30 a.m. the morning before. I had to play mean aunt and scold them before my sister got up. I did not like to discipline other people's children, but it was better than the alternative: Teresa scolding them. And to the eighth power. That would have been much worse.

When my cell phone vibrated on my desk, I was happy to look over and see my brother Frankie's face beaming on the screen. We had been texting and sending each other photos from the weekend all morning. He was the first one up yesterday at 4:30 in the morning. I wondered how he was getting along on his day. "Heeeeeeyyy, Beaner, what's up?" I tilted back in my chair with a big, lazy smile on my face.

"Annie?" He sounded both serious and confused, probably wondering why I sounded so playful. He must have realized I didn't know yet. "Yeah, what's up?" I asked. And then he said it, the two most unimaginable words together in one sentence:

"Teresa's dead."

"Whaaaat?" I screamed in horror into the phone. "Who told you that?" I demanded. "Pat said that you told him," he defended. "I didn't tell him that!" I argued. "You've got it wrong, Bean! I didn't tell Pat anything! This is a mistake. I'm going to call Pat."

I hung up and immediately called my other brother to get to the bottom of this confusion. But when he answered the phone, I knew it was true. "Hey," he said in between gasps of tears. "Pat! What's going on? Frankie just called and said I told you Teresa is dead. What are you talking about?" I demanded. "She's dead, Ann," he managed to reply through his tears. "No, she can't be, because Frankie said I told you, and I didn't, so she can't be dead because I never said that," I insisted, as if I could change anything he was going to say. "Mom told me. I must have been so upset that I told him it was you."

I started crying and screaming, "Oh my God! No! Teresa's dead?" Several friends in my department swarmed my cube. Jenn and Deborah put their hands on my arms.

"How could she be dead? What happened?" I screamed at my brother in disbelief. I could feel my heart pounding. "I don't know anything, Ann." "Where's Mom?" I asked. He told me she was on her way to Florida with Mark and the kids. What? I couldn't imagine the state my mother was in. How could she be on a plane? Her daughter was dead. Her precious Teresa was dead. I cried harder. My poor mother.

My mind jumped between imagining my life without my sister and worrying about my mother. And then the kids? "Oh my God! The kids! Did they tell Jo and Carm?" Pat repeated the same thing to every question I bombarded him with. "Honey, I don't know anything more."

I hung up the phone and tried my mother anyway. Maybe I could catch her, but it went straight to voicemail. I started to call Teresa, because who else would I call in a moment like this? The reality was crushing. I could never call her again.

I called my best friend, Karen. I knew she couldn't be on her cell phone at work, but I felt strongly that she would answer and was surprised and grateful when she did. "Hey, what's up?" she asked, surprised and curious. "Teresa's dead." A moment of silence, and then very softly and lovingly, she asked, "Do you want me to come to you?" "Yes. I need you," I said. I hung up the phone and stood there. Lost.

The next thing I knew, my boss, Carl, was driving me in my car to my house while Deborah and Jenn followed behind. I was embarrassed that my car was a mess, and in the next second, I remembered my sister was dead. Random, monotonous thoughts entered my mind, each one eclipsed with a reminder that Teresa was dead until I was consumed with that thought alone.

I rested my head on the window and looked at the world outside without my sister in it. How could she be dead? She was a powerhouse, the healthiest person I knew. Nothing got her down. She was about to reach the masses. And what about our mission? We were supposed to do something really big together. All the signs had pointed to that. What did "Aquarius" mean? How can there be a mission if Teresa is dead?

Carl interrupted my thoughts. Poor guy. It must have been hard for him to watch me. He knew how much my sister meant to me. He had allowed me to work remotely countless times so that I could be with her for long weekends. He started to ask questions. When did my sister get home? When did I talk to her last? I sat there like a zombie, robotically answering his questions. Where were her kids and her husband? How did she get home from the airport? I told him that we had all returned home the day before, but Teresa's husband and children stayed behind to spend some time in Connecticut. I knew

Teresa had arrived at the airport in New York around 5:30 p.m. She'd called me.

I was just about to sit down and eat, so we only talked for a minute. Why didn't I just let my food get cold? Maybe I could have prevented this from happening? My head was dizzy with what-ifs.

When we pulled into my driveway, my son was already standing outside waiting for me. My beautiful nineteen-year-old son, with his shoulder-length auburn hair, stared at me as I approached him. I could see the concern in his intense dark eyes as they locked into mine. He was searching my face. He didn't look sad, he looked scared, because he already understood that the mother he had known was gone. Like everyone else who knew me, he, too, had already begun calculating the impact Teresa's death would have on me. We reached for each other, and he hugged me tightly. We released and went back to staring at each other. There were no words. I had stopped crying, but I was in shock. "I need a cigarette. Could you go get me some?" I asked blankly. Mick knew I had quit but didn't protest. "Of course."

I guess I introduced everyone to my son, but I don't remember. Carl, Jenn, and Deborah followed me through my kitchen, dark dining room, and living room, past the bar, through the sliders to my studio, and out to the back patio. We sat down on my old patio furniture. Carl continued asking questions, "What part of Florida does your sister live in? I know some people in law enforcement down there. Maybe I could get some answers." I told him she lived in Bonita Springs and her medical practice was in Estero.

I got up and went to the bar in my living room and poured myself a glass of Jack Daniels. *So this is how we were going to do it, Annie? Cigarettes and booze? Yep. This is how we're doing it.* I returned to the table, whiskey in hand, and lit up a cigarette with no regard for the non-smokers around me. I didn't care that they saw me smoking or drinking. My walls were down and I felt myself slipping away, growing stiller and more silent as I repeated the same two thoughts.

What happened? What am I going to do without her?

I was interrupted when I heard the sound of the screen door bursting open from the studio out to the patio. It was my brother, Patrick. His face and eyes were red as he cried shamelessly in front of these strangers in my backyard. I ran up to him. We stood there for a long time holding each other, crying and muffling into each other's shoulders, "I can't believe she's gone."

Hours went by with no answers. I made phone calls to aunts, uncles, cousins, and friends. People started to arrive at the house. Aunt Rita was there with a couple of trays of food and pastries. Karen took over my kitchen and was preparing all kinds of food. My stepmother, Oma, put on a pot of coffee. I couldn't believe how quickly people had gotten there. They were everywhere: in the kitchen, dining room, and living room, the front yard, back patio, and front porch. I was grateful to be surrounded by so much love that I desperately needed.

By this time, Carl, Jenn, and Deborah had left to head back to the office. Carl had told me he would let me know if he heard anything from his friend from Florida, and I told them I would let them know if I heard anything.

I was in my living room sitting on the floor in front of the two large drawers of my entertainment center. Patrick sat behind me on the sofa. I pulled opened the bottom drawer, not really believing what I was about to do. My hands reached in and pulled out various photo albums and envelopes filled with pictures. I plopped them in front of me and started going through the photos. I needed to see her. I needed to see that it was real once—that she had lived.

I found pictures of her that used to make me laugh so hard: the one with Teresa standing between my uncle Pete and cousin Petey. She was laughing with a fat cigar clenched in her teeth. I turned around and flashed it to Pat, who was lost in his thoughts on the sofa. He gave a soft laugh and quickly fell silent. I put the photo aside, thinking I should save it for the slideshow at the funeral home.

How was this happening? Was I really gathering photos for my sister's wake? How was I going to plan a wake? Would we have to go to Florida? Would I have to have two services to accommodate two states? Before I could even begin to answer these random questions that were invading my thoughts, I was interrupted by Patrick's cell phone. "Hey, Bean," I heard him say softly.

It was Frankie. I wondered if he was heading to Connecticut yet, but before I could finish my thought, Pat's scream broke the silence. "No! No!" In an instant, I knew I was about to find out what had happened to my sister, and I knew it was going to be something horrible. "Get your computer!" Pat cried impatiently.

I grabbed my computer and typed in the web address that Pat was repeating as Frankie spelled it out to him. The screen opened, and to my horror, I saw my sister's home covered with crime scene tape and crawling with police officers. Standing in front of her house was a beautiful anchorwoman speaking into a microphone. "I am standing in front of the home of Dr. Teresa Sievers, who was found murdered this morning in her Bonita Springs home. Neighbors report the scene was gruesome."

Murdered? Gruesome? Those were terrifying words. I screamed, repeating over and over, "I'll never sleep again!" I had to run. I needed to throw something. I had to get out of there. I headed toward my studio to make way for the back patio. Glasses and decanters on the bar caught my attention as I approached the sliding door to my studio.

Without a thought, I sliced my hand through rows of glasses and barware.

I ran outside and stared at the sky. In my mind, I screamed at God! How could you let this happen? I sobbed from the deepest part of my soul. I couldn't catch my breath.

Screams erupted from various places inside and outside of the house as the news of Teresa's murder spread to family and friends.

The nightmare had only just begun.

Chapter 28

My Sister Was Murdered

Remember my soundtrack, Ode to Joy? Well, for those of you who date back to vinyl, imagine listening to the peak of the chorus at full volume. Now imagine someone unplugging the turntable and the distorted lyrics slowly descending, losing their pitch, and plummeting to an unbearable bass note before silence.

My sister was murdered. The scene was gruesome.

The next day I was standing at the airport bar in Hartford with my brothers. It was early. My bestie Karen had packed some clothes for me. The previous day was already a blur. I looked around at the people sitting at the bar drinking 7:00 a.m. cocktails before they headed to their gates. That definitely wasn't for me. I needed focus and strength, and that was already in short supply.

The three of us were on our phones checking messages and searching the Internet for any updates on the murder. Frankie found something. He tilted his phone screen toward Pat and me. A gurney with a black body bag on top rolled out of my sister's house.

My sister was murdered. The scene was gruesome.

My Teresa. My girl. Her beautiful body was inside that black bag. My knees buckled, and I started to go down, but my brother Frankie steadied me to my feet.

My sadness quickly changed to anger. How can people be so heartless? Don't they know that her family is going to see this? Her mother is going to see this! But considering I learned about my sister's murder from a news report the day before, I shouldn't have been surprised. And this was just the beginning.

There would be more images. Worse images.

My sister was murdered. It was gruesome.

Chapter 29

Alive and Kicking

I've read countless books and listened to twice as many podcasts about our multi-dimensional nature. My favorite topic is life after death, consciousness. I am so grateful to people who have had the courage to share their experiences with humanity.

One of the most widely recognized spiritual mediums, James Van Praagh—my personal favorite—wrote several incredible books that document his many remarkable experiences as a psychic medium. James is absolute when he explains that almost from the moment we exit this physical dimension, we are standing right beside our beloveds in spirit form, emphatically repeating, "I'm not dead. I'm still here."

Our beloveds will use any vehicle they can to get our attention. As pure energy, it's easy for them to tap into electronics, causing lights to flicker, appliances and electronics to turn on and off. Some will leave coins around.

Some will plant an idea or a song in your head.

It was our third day in Florida. After a couple of nights in a hotel, we managed to find two condo units in the same complex to accommodate our family and extended family who would arrive during the week.

One morning after breakfast before we each headed out with our to-do lists, I was sitting with my brother Patrick. "I have a song stuck in my head, and it's driving me crazy." I asked him the name of the song, but he said he couldn't remember. "I just know it's by Simple Minds. I don't know why it's stuck in my head. I haven't heard the song in years. And I don't even like it. Isn't that weird?"

Later that night when we regrouped for dinner, Pat excitedly gathered everyone around, "You guys aren't going to believe what happened!" He filled everyone in about the song that had invaded his head space. "Well," he continued, "it was so annoying." A few people asked what the name of the song was. "That was another thing. I knew the song, but for the life of me I couldn't remember the title," Pat said.

I had the feeling I knew where my brother was going with this. This sounded very similar to an experience I had years back in the beginning of my mystical journey with Lois.

Pat continued with his story, "Anyway, Frankie and I stopped off to grab some wine at some random liquor store we found in our travels, and as soon as we walked in the door, that song was playing!"

The song is called "Alive and Kicking."

We knew at once it was Teresa.

She was alive.

And she was kicking.

Chapter 30

Lyin' Eyes

It's the husband. That's what people were saying. Either in hushed tones around the family or on any online crime forum.

It's the husband.

I didn't believe that. Mark was weird. Mark was creepy. But a murderer? Kill the mother of his children? For what? Even when the police interviewed me, I said—and I cringe every time that video pops up on my YouTube feed—"Mark worshiped the ground Teresa walked on."

Well, that's what Mark wanted us to believe anyway. And it worked for a while.

Besides, Mark was in Connecticut with the kids. They were staying at my mother's house.

One night at my rented condo, my brothers, a few cousins and close friends, and I sat around the dining room table drinking wine. I had been in Florida for about five days, and the memorial service was the following morning.

Pat was the first one to say it out loud: "Have you guys noticed how weird Mark is acting?" What else is new, I thought. "Pat, Mark is weird," I said.

"But haven't you noticed that he doesn't have any tears in his eyes when he is crying?"

Daniele and Frankie shrieked, "Yes!"

I had noticed it, too, but I had witnessed lots of bizarre behavior from this guy. Who knows? Maybe he had an issue with his tear ducts? Maybe he simply couldn't cry? Maybe he was in shock?

Maybe he was a psychopath?

Someone asked the room, "Do you guys think he did it?"

"No way," I said. "There's no way Mark would ever hurt Teresa." He's just inappropriate sometimes. He's a goofball. He's socially awkward.

Maybe he was a psychopath?

"I don't know, Ann. What about the night he came to our hotel room?" Daniele was looking at me and then turned to the group. "The night I arrived, he knocked on our door at midnight! Annie and I were already in bed."

They spoke quietly near the door, so I couldn't hear what they were saying. Not wanting to deal with Mark, I pretended to be asleep. I knew Daniele could handle him for me. I was so exhausted I just passed out.

Daniele continued, "He appeared to be crying. His body was shaking. He was making noises as if he were crying. But there were no tears. It was really weird. It looked like he was faking, but like Annie said, Mark is weird. So, I didn't overthink it."

Daniele expected Mark to tell her how broken he was, how he didn't know how he would go on without Teresa. She thought they would share their grief together. Cry together. Or that they would try and figure out what happened to Teresa. Who killed her? Why was nothing stolen? The money and jewelry that lay in plain sight. The shear brutality of it all.

He spoke of none of those things.

Instead, Mark wanted Daniele to assure him that if anything happened to him, she would make sure the girls were taken care of according to his and Teresa's will and irrevocable trust.

Where was Mark going? Was he going somewhere?

Next, Mark wanted to talk about money.

If Mark had a favorite topic, it was money. He was the kind of guy who knew how much money he had in his wallet at all times. He was the kind of guy who would drive an extra ten miles to get a half gallon of milk twenty cents cheaper. He was the kind of guy who wrote off anything he possibly could as a business expense, right down to a candy bar from a vending machine.

He was that guy. And we all knew it.

So when Daniele told us Mark said he no idea how much life insurance there was on Teresa, suspicions grew. None of us knew exactly how much, but we knew there was at least several million.

And so did Mark.

"Mark couldn't remember anything, you guys. Teresa bitched about it all the time. Don't you remember how crazy that made her? He was just forgetful."

Was he?

One by one, my brothers, cousins, and friends weighed in on their off-beat interactions with Mark.

"What about what he did at the funeral home?" Karen finally spoke up. Everyone turned to look at Karen. She had been sitting in the corner quietly, observing as was her style. "I was standing next to Annie, and he walked right up to me and said, 'You must be Karen.' Then he put his arms around my waist, slid his hand down to my ass, and kissed me on the lips."

While the mortician was putting his wife's head back together downstairs.

All of it was unsettling and suspicious, but I just couldn't conceive of it.

Finally, we went around the table and took a vote to see who thought Mark did it. I voted no. "Why would Mark kill the mother of his children just as she was about to become a household name?" I asked the room.

Silence.

No one could come up with a motive.

Not on that night.

Chapter 31

A Funeral in My Life

In between police inquiries and a couple of interviews with the local media—which I quickly put an end to once I saw how they twisted my words—I had to plan my sister's memorial service. I directed the sad occasion as if it were a show, complete with a call sheet for music cues, slides, videos, and eulogies. I wanted it to be perfect.

After the slideshow and before the processional, the music was supposed to stop, and video clips of Teresa were supposed to begin. But the DVD wasn't working. There was no visual, but the audio played through the sound system. In the silence that followed after the music stopped, my sister's voice boomed through the church, "Hi. I'm Dr. Teresa Sievers. Hi. I'm Dr. Teresa Sievers," over and over again. It was weird. Unsettling.

And it made Mark furious. He was standing in front of me with the kids at the entrance of the church when he made a beeline for the audiovisual technician. Then he yelled at the technician. Inside the quiet church.

"Turn that thing off now!"

Hmm.

Mark's best friend, Curtis "Wayne" Wright, had his own peculiar reaction to the sound of Teresa's voice amplified through the church's rather impressive sound system. Lucky for Wayne, or perhaps not, Teresa's dear friend, Beth, one of several doctors in attendance, was sent for by Mark after the service. Wayne told Beth he suffered from asthma and couldn't breathe. Beth told me later that it wasn't asthma.

Wayne was suffering from a panic attack.

Hmm.

I didn't care much about the video. For me, the music was the most important. I planned to have "In My Life" by the Beatles play after I read my eulogy. That was my and Teresa's song. We had claimed it in July of 1991 right before she left the country for medical school.

It was only a couple of weeks before Teresa traveled far away to Dominica to medical school. The fun we had living together on the second floor of our family home was about to come to an end. Those days were some of the best times of our lives. We hadn't spent that much time together since before she left for college. Our relationship and bond had deepened to a new level.

Teresa and I got pretty clingy as her departure date approached. We were closer than ever and couldn't bear the thought of being separated. We took advantage of every moment of the time we had left, somehow knowing there would never be another time in our lives like it—a time with virtually unlimited access to each other.

A couple of weeks before she left, we sat together in my car in a parking lot somewhere in between running errands for her departure and my wedding. We were listening to the Beatles "Rubber Soul," a CD that played endlessly that summer. As we began singing along to "In My Life," we both burst into tears. I remember how tightly we hugged each other as the lyrics underscored the depths of our affection. "In my life I love you more." When the song finished, Teresa said, quite powerfully, "This is our song!" I laughed because she said it as if John and Paul had written it just for us. She could be so intense, that

Teresa! But, of course, I couldn't think of a better song to define our relationship. "Yes!" I said. "It's perfect."

Two weeks later, as maid of honor at my second wedding, we took to the dance floor for a special dance I had designated just for the two of us. Friends and family gathered around to watch, most of them with tears in their eyes. Our love vibrated through that reception hall.

Now, many of the same people who watched us sway together on the dance floor all those years ago stared up at me as I stood at the pulpit with a larger-than-life portrait of my sister projected next to me.

I finished my eulogy, and "In My Life" began right on cue. I don't know why, but I turned toward the screen with one hand on my heart and the other raised toward her. I didn't plan on doing that; it just happened. It felt right. When I repeated this dedication in Connecticut, a friend told me that everyone in the audience had also placed their hand on their heart and raised their hand to Teresa as well. I was very touched by that.

About a month after Teresa's death, Petr and I visited Zito in New Jersey. It was a somber time, but the visit involved a special weekend that had been planned for a long time to see one of my and Zito's favorite bands, Tedeschi Trucks. The weekend was so strange. There I was with my best friend at a concert watching a performer who inspired our set list for years. I was surrounded by people I loved at a concert that normally would have had me ten feet off the ground. But I was so weighed down with grief, I couldn't feel anything.

Zito was broken up too. He adored Teresa and gave a beautiful eulogy for her at the Florida service. Zito had explained to everyone gathered at Unity Church how he knew Teresa. "When I became friends with Annie, it was like I got the two-for-one deal. Teresa was automatically a part of the package. I loved Teresa."

Teresa adored Zito as much as I did. Zito once said to me, "Do you realize your sister cannot say my name without swearing?" It was always, "Fucking Zito," as in, "Fucking Zito, I love you." Or when she took Zito on as a patient and was reviewing his food log, "Fucking Zito, you're killing me with the Cheerios for breakfast."

Like I said, my sister loved to swear.

After the concert, we stopped for a bite at a cafeteria-style restaurant. Petr and I sat down with our trays first. As we waited for Zito and his wife to be seated, I listened to the piped-in music overhead. The song that was playing stopped abruptly. I couldn't believe what I now heard.

It was the unmistakable harpsichord intro of "In My Life."

Zito approached the table, staring at me as he sat down. "Yep. I hear it, Annie." It was profound and painful. Zito brought levity, "Fucking Teresa."

A few weeks later, I met my dear friend Cindy for lunch. Cindy was another lucky recipient of the two-for-one package. When I arrived at the restaurant, Cindy was waiting for me in the foyer. I thought she was crying because of the obvious. When I pulled away from her embrace, she pointed her finger up and said, "Can't you hear it? Teresa is welcoming us," she said as "In My Life" played overhead in the restaurant foyer.

I closed my eyes and remembered that day we sat together, hugging in my car. Teresa picked the perfect lyrics to encapsulate our timeless affection for one another: "Some are dead and some are living. In my life I love you more."

Chapter 32

Lost

I woke up the morning after the memorial service exhausted and emotional. I had been so busy planning and coordinating the services that I didn't have time to be sad. I didn't have time to project into the future—a future without my sister. Now, as I sat on the bedroom floor of the rented condo, I attempted to imagine the future.

I saw nothing.

I reached over to pick up one of the mass cards that lay on top of my suitcase and looked at my sister's face. The photo was nothing short of magnificent. There had never been a photo like it that captured my sister's light and beauty so exquisitely. The picture was from a professional photo shoot she had done several months earlier. But instead of branding her television show or the book she was working on, it became the famous photo that eventually everyone in the world would associate with the murdered doctor from Southwest Florida.

I stared at her picture and willed her to speak to me. To scold me. Anything. I didn't know what to do. I needed her to tell me what to do. In a situation like this, Teresa would take control. She'd know what to do next, and she would be telling everyone what needed to be done. I didn't know where to begin. I stared deeper into the picture.

"Tell me what to do. Please tell me what to do, Tre, because I don't know how to go on without you telling me what to do." I was surprised when an image of Teresa's dogs emerged through my sadness.

"Why am I thinking about your dogs?" I asked her in my mind, and then I immediately understood. Of course! Your dogs. Those poor dogs. They were in the house somewhere when my sister was attacked. The thought made me sick. They were getting fed daily, but that was all. She was right. I needed to get those dogs out of that house, but I had no idea who could take them.

Suddenly, I remembered a woman at the memorial service had specifically offered to help me find a place for the dogs. I don't know how she knew about the dogs, and I couldn't remember her name. She had handed me her business card at the service. I remembered putting the card in a white drawstring bag that one of the women from the church gave me to place the cards in that people handed me.

I looked around the room and rummaged through my things, but I didn't have the bag. I assumed I must have left it at the church. "Okay," I said as I looked back at my sister's picture, "I'm going to call the church and get that woman's card so we can get your girlies out of that house."

I grabbed my cell, stepped outside for a signal, and waited patiently as I listened to the menu options. "If you'd like to leave a message or make an appointment for the crystal healing bed . . ." *Crystal healing bed? Waaaait a minute.* That got my attention immediately.

Teresa had mentioned something about getting a crystal healing bed for her patients. She told me that crystals have powerful healing properties. So that's what this was about. She knew I was in desperate need of healing and knew the dogs would lead me to that woman and then to the church. I knew my sister was guiding me. I felt as if I'd just hung up the phone with her when I burst out of the bedroom and into the kitchen. I exuded excitement as I told my mother what happened.

"Mom, the crystal healing bed is like a Reiki session on steroids." The only thing my mother knew about Reiki was that I had studied it and Teresa had a Reiki practitioner in her office. I quickly explained how Reiki cleared blockages in the chakras to promote physical, emotional, and spiritual healing.

The word Chakra dates back between 1500 to 1000 BC, where they were first mentioned in the Vedas, which are ancient sacred texts of spiritual knowledge. Chakras are spinning disks of energy that correspond to our nerves, organs, and energetic body and affect our emotional and physical well-being. These energy centers need to remain open and aligned to maintain physical and emotional well-being. Unreleased anger, grief, or any fear-based emotion—negative energy—blocks the energy flow and leads to emotional and physical illness. I was surprised when she said, "I'd like to go on that crystal healing bed too."

Ahh. There was more. *That* was it. The thoughts came through to me quickly and clearly.

My mother needed the healing bed. I understood that instantly.

Then something else became immediately clear.

The crystal healing bed was at Unity Church, where the lovely Reverend Diane had celebrated my sister's mass the day before. Reverend Diane had been a great comfort to my mother over the past week. My mother felt very peaceful when she was with her. I knew what I had to do.

I called Reverend Diane directly and asked her to be with us during our crystal healing bed session. I told her I needed her to hold space for my mother because I had to have a very difficult conversation with my mother, a conversation that I very much dreaded.

I needed to tell my mother what happened to her daughter when she arrived home on June 28.

My brothers and I had struggled with how to go about that. None of us could imagine having that conversation with my mother, but we had to do something soon. It would be all over the news at any moment, and I couldn't let my mother find out like that.

It was Mark who told us the police asked if he kept a ball peen hammer in the garage. I remember the stupid look on his face as he feigned ignorance about what types of hammers he had in his tool inventory, as if to suggest he wouldn't know one type of hammer from another, nor why the police would ask him such a question.

No one came out and said the words. It was too horrible to imagine. I didn't know what happened to my sister when she walked into her house that night. But when I was told the funeral director would need time to work on my sister, I thought, well, this guy must know. He hesitated to answer me when I asked him, "How many times?"

Yes. I knew this was the reason my sister made me think about her dogs. It was also why I'd left the drawstring bag filled with cards at the church. And the reason my sister talked about crystal healing beds last September in Newark.

Wait! September in Newark?

Yes! September 28. I could never forget that date. It was our last night alone together on earth. It was the night we found out we had a mission.

And then it hit me.

The 28th of *June* was Teresa's last night on earth. Before I even finished counting the months, I knew the timing would be significant. Teresa was murdered exactly to the day, nine months after we discovered our mission. Somehow the metaphor of birth and creation resonated with me. Years later, when the mission unfolded, I would understand its meaning.

But the multiple, synchronistic epiphanies that unfolded in rapid succession the moment I called Unity Church did not escape me. I knew what they meant.

Teresa was still with me, and she was still telling me what to do.

The next day we made our way back to Unity Church. I hadn't had time to take in the beauty of the property when we were there two days earlier. It looked like a nature preserve surrounded by lush vegetation and tropical flowers, with birdsong in the air. It felt peaceful and holy.

Reverend Diane welcomed my mother and me and as we entered a small room in a building adjacent to the church. Her energy was nothing but kind and loving as she embraced my mother, who immediately began to sob in her arms. My poor, sweet mother. How on earth was I going to do this?

Eventually, Reverend Diane led us to a small table. We began with a prayer, which put Mom at ease. After a moment, I began, "Mom, I need to talk to you about what happened to Teresa. I'm not sure what you've heard." My mother was tentative and weepy. "I heard something about a hammer. Did someone hit her with a hammer?" she asked with the innocence of a child. I nodded.

"Mom, if I could protect you from hearing the rest, I would, but it's going to be all over the news very soon. And I thought this would be the best way to tell you. My mother looked down at her hands and nodded her head. "Okay," she said softly.

As gently and respectfully as I could, I told my mother that Teresa was hit in the head with a hammer.

"How many times?" Mom asked.

I choked as I said, "Seventeen."

I quickly wrapped my arms around her, holding her as tightly as I could, "But, Mom, she was killed instantly." I didn't know if that was true, but we both needed to believe that it was.

Four and a half years later, at the first of two murder trials, my mother and I sat in a courtroom as Curtis Wayne Wright described what happened the night he hid in my sister's garage waiting for her to come home. The fact was that my sister fought for her life until she couldn't any longer.

About a year later I read a book about past life regressions. In it, I learned that when the physical body is experiencing severe trauma, the spirit leaves the body to protect it from pain.

I hold on to that still.

Chapter 33

It's the Husband

I remember looking at my mother sitting in the front row as I read my eulogy at Teresa's Connecticut memorial service. She sat calmly and full of grace. It struck me so profoundly that I went off script. "I always thought I got my strength from my father," I said to the crowd of people gathered in the high school auditorium where years ago Teresa had graduated valedictorian. "But I can see now that it's been my mother all along. Mom, you're amazing."

It was the day after the crystal healing bed. Most people had left for home. I sat at the dining room table with my mother who, after going through the worst any parent could imagine, was prepared to remain in Florida indefinitely with her grandchildren. Mom's husband sat with us as did my brother Frankie. We were waiting for Mark to return from a meeting with his lawyer. We were all anxious to hear about it. Why did Mark need a lawyer anyway?

Annie, can you say denial?

Since we were all gathered, I also wanted to discuss an exit plan for Mom. I didn't want my mother to remain in Florida. I wanted to get back to Connecticut. "Mom, it will be an absolute shit show down here. I know you don't want to leave the kids, but if you stay here you will have deal with Mark." My mother loved Mark, but like my sister and everyone else, he annoyed her. His disorganization and forgetfulness could be the undoing of my mother. Strong as she was, I knew how he could get on my nerves, and I didn't want my mother to have to deal with that.

She protested. "Ann Marie, I cannot leave my grandchildren." She was resigned. I knew it. She called me by my first and middle name. I didn't want to fight with her, but there was absolutely no way I was going to leave Florida without her. "Mom, believe me when I tell you, Teresa does not want you to deal with Mark. He will drive you nuts. I know this. *I feel this!* Besides, Mark's mother is here, and his brother is coming back this weekend. They can help Mark with the kids, Mom. And let's be honest, this hasn't even hit you yet. I don't want you to be walking through an airport alone or trapped on a plane next to some stranger when it does."

This is not the time to Tottenize my mother.

Frankie and Tom chimed in, in agreement, especially with regard to Mom traveling solo. Slowly, my mother began to nod her head. I could tell she was starting to see the big picture, to see the light. She knew I was right. I suggested we take the kids back to Connecticut with us. That would give Mark time to deal with the insurance companies and take care of Teresa's medical practice. There were patients who needed referrals and many who needed supplements or special prescriptions. My mother loved that idea. We could take care of the kids and not have to deal with Mark. Our exit plan was in place.

Or so we thought.

An hour later, Mark returned from his meeting with his lawyer. He was uncharacteristically quiet, his goofy demeanor replaced with a seriousness like none of us had ever witnessed. According to Mark, his lawyer squashed Mark's plans to move back into the house. The lawyer said it wouldn't look good.

No shit, really, Mark?

Mark had been talking about moving back into his house with the kids long before the crime scene tape was removed. Of course, we all thought this was beyond fucked-up. How on earth could he ever live in that house again? Eat in that kitchen? The kitchen where my sister made the most delicious gluten-free, dairy-free gourmet dishes. The kitchen where the kids sat at the counter drinking their green smoothies. The kitchen where she danced in her underwear singing along with Mary J. Blige blasting at full volume. The kitchen where the mother of his children was found face down in front of the refrigerator in a pool of blood after being bludgeoned to death by seventeen blows from a ball peen hammer.

How is it that we did not catch on? How did we not know that under the facade of mindlessness and feigning ignorance and forgetfulness, there was a conniving, manipulative psychopath?

After Mark finished telling us about the rest of his meeting with his lawyer, I broached the subject of the kids. I explained my concerns about not wanting to leave Mom in Florida and suggested we take the kids to Connecticut to get away from the scene and the media that was lurking everywhere.

"Annie, I don't want those kids anywhere but with me." Mark's tone was very direct and very serious. I had never heard this tone before. It was unsettling. It was very un-Mark. I tried again.

"But, Mark, if we brought them to Connecticut, they could be with the cousins and just be kids for a while." I could see he was becoming agitated with me. "It's not all fun and games, Annie. The kids have homeschool, violin and karate, and other obligations. Life needs to get back to normal." Really, dude? Like it's ever going to be normal again,

I thought. I tried one more time, "We could find a violin teacher in Connecticut and get a homeschool . . ."

Mark slammed his fist on the table. Now he was yelling at me, "Annie you're not listening to me! Those kids are not going anywhere! They are staying here with me, and that's final!"

I glanced at my mother and Frankie. I could tell they were as shocked by Mark's behavior as I was. Finally, I acquiesced, but told him that Mom would be returning home with me the day after next. Then I got up from the table and headed to my room.

Frankie caught up beside me. "Jesus!" I said half-jokingly. "Talk about taking the kids, and the guy goes crazy." I had barely gotten the words out of my mouth. "Oh my God!" I whispered. I turned to my brother and grabbed him by the shoulder. "He did it! She was going to divorce him and take the kids! So he killed her!"

I pulled Frankie into my room and shut the door. "Jesus!" Frankie said. "For the past week we've been telling him everything the police told us about the investigation. We're going to have to try to continue to act as though we don't suspect him. The slightest inconsistency, and that bastard will know that we're on to him."

We were both so freaked out.

I didn't know who to call or what to do next, and before I could figure it out, there was a knock on my bedroom door. Frankie opened it.

There was Mark Sievers right on cue.

"What are you guys doing?" he asked in his creepy Mark Sievers' voice.

It was as if he knew he blew it when he broke character and lost his temper, and now he was evaluating the fallout. "Oh, nothing," Frankie said, trying to act normal. "Annie and I are just trying to figure out when she and Mom will head back." Mark stared at Frankie; he looked suspicious. "But Annie just said she was going back the day after tomorrow." I jumped in quickly, "He just meant we were trying to figure out what time we should leave and when to return the rental and all that." I was so nervous. I could feel myself starting to sweat.

Mark came into the room and sat at the head of the bed, and Frankie followed, sitting at the foot, with me on the floor beneath him. Mark sat there cooly, not taking his eyes off either of us. I can't remember exactly what he said, but he started talking about the murder investigation. Stuff like, "And the police said this . . ." and, "What do you guys know about that . . . ?" Without thinking, I started to answer his questions. I was trying so hard to act normal that I forgot that I needed to keep my mouth shut. I felt Frankie kicking my thigh with his foot as if to say *would you shut the fuck up already.*

But Frankie was snagged.

Mark saw Frankie kicking me, and I cannot emphasize enough this man's creepy voice: "Frankie, why are you kicking Annie?" Before Frankie could answer, I snapped out of it and got right into character. "Yeah, Frank, could you stop kicking me please?" Luckily Frankie caught on. "Oh, I'm sorry, I was stretching my legs and didn't even realize I was hitting you with my foot. Sorry." Mark seemed to fall for it. We talked for a while longer, Frank and I both feigning allegiance to Mark. After a while, Mark said good night and left. God only knows what he's up to, I thought.

Frank and I struggled with what to do next. We agreed that we needed to call the police. But were we sure? Were we 100 percent completely, absolutely, positively sure he did it? I didn't want to believe it. I was at

99.9, but I knew I couldn't have even the tiniest doubt before I sent my niece's and nephew's father to prison for murder.

By the time Frankie left, my mother and her husband had gone up to bed. I was alone. For the first time since I learned about my sister's murder, I was alone, and I was going to be sleeping alone too. No husband. No friends. No family.

Shit! Mark knows I'm alone!

Of course he did. He may have acted like he had no idea what was going on, but that son of a bitch knew I was alone.

Oh my God! What if he comes back?

It would be just like him to knock on the door at midnight just like he did that night at the hotel. I had never had a panic attack before, but I was pretty sure I was having one. I needed to call someone. I needed someone to tell me I was right. I needed to solidify what I believed to be Mark's motive. But it was late. There had to be someone who was still up! I thought for a minute. Aunt Mary! She'll be up.

Mary was my dad's sister and Teresa's godmother, and a confidant to us sisters. Teresa and I could tell Aunt Mary things that we weren't ready to share with each other. You know, those things that you didn't want your sister to throw in your face or be held accountable for? Like if Teresa had absolutely had it with her husband, or that she was wondering where all of her money was. Or maybe that she was going to file for divorce. Those kinds of things. Because if she told me, her sister, soulmate, life coach, and cheerleader any of those things and then chickened out in the end, I would have to hold her accountable. I'd have to start asking her questions, like, "How can you still be married to a guy who is embezzling your money?" Teresa wouldn't have been able to show up at a family gathering—say New York for our mom's seventy-fifth birthday—and look me in the face.

Nope. Better not tell your sister this one. Panicked and paranoid, I grabbed my cell phone and charged outside for a signal to call Aunt Mary.

***

I had been right. Teresa let it all out with Aunt Mary. She told Aunt Mary she couldn't do it anymore. Teresa told our aunt that Mark was sucking the life out of her. She even talked about divorce, something she had never done before. I was now 100 percent sure that Mark Sievers had a motive to murder my sister. Now I needed to be 100 percent sure that he did it.

And I knew just who to ask.

Teresa.

Chapter 34

Dirty Deeds Done Dirt Cheap

Two days after I realized that Mark had motive to kill my sister, Mom and I were at the airport and ready to head back home. But there would be no respite for us. We had another memorial service to plan for our family and friends in Connecticut. Media outlets were texting and calling to request interviews. I didn't know what to do first. My head was spinning. I wanted to call investigators, but I needed to figure things out.

I needed to talk to Teresa.

She was the only one who could confirm my strong convictions about Mark. I needed to hear it from her. I needed her to give me a sign. A color. A yes or no. Two pennies. Something. But what little energy I had was scattered, and I knew that would make it very difficult to connect with her. So I reached out to my bestie, Karen, or as I called her, my wife from another life, for help.

I've always believed that Karen and I were married in a past life. The dynamics of our long friendship were very much like two old souls who'd spent at least one lifetime married to each other. I had shared this intuition with Teresa years ago, who, having played "marriage counselor" for me over the years, agreed wholeheartedly. "Yeah, you two have some karma to figure out." Of course, I had no way to prove that. I just knew it. I wouldn't know the extent of my soul connection until after I died.

Or until someone close to me died and found a way to tell me. Like Teresa. And naturally she found a rather interesting way to tell me.

It was the night I learned about Teresa's murder. Everyone had left my house, Karen came looking for me and found me in my studio. "I need to tell you something," she said very seriously but softly.

I've known Karen since I was eleven years old, and I could tell by the look in her eyes that she was about to tell me that something really weird had happened.

"Something really weird happened," she began.

I knew it!

"I was awakened from my sleep last night by someone rubbing my back in the middle of the night."

She said it had probably happened sometime between 11:30 and 12:30. "Annie, you know I sleep alone with the door locked." I asked her if she thought it was Teresa. "That's what I am wondering now, but why would she come to me? Why wouldn't she have gone to you?" Karen was right. Teresa and Karen had no relationship whatsoever. In fact, it would be fair to say that they clashed. I was dumbfounded. It didn't make any sense.

Until the same thing happened to me two nights later. I somehow intuited that the order of the back rubs was Teresa's way of letting me know that Karen and I definitely had a significant past life relationship. And that perhaps, Teresa felt closer to Karen now that she was on the other side.

That's how I decided that I could ask Karen for help.

So before Mom and I boarded our plane back to Connecticut, I called Karen, "I need you to ask Teresa for a sign." Karen was confused. "Me? Why don't you?" I explained what happened with Mark at the condo the night before. "Kar, my energy is so frenetic. You can take the time to get yourself centered. You know you can do this..."

"Why would Teresa tell me?" Karen asked confused. "Because," I said. "Teresa knows we were married in a past life. That's why she rubbed your back first. That was her way of telling me."

"How do you know that?" Karen asked.

"I just *know*! I can't explain it, Karen. Anyway, I'm too frenetic right now. I don't know if Teresa will be able to get through to me. Besides, you are so intuitive, and Teresa knows that."

And like a good wife, Karen agreed to ask Teresa for a sign.

I'd never been so happy to sit in a plane. I was so exhausted I collapsed in the seat with my mother next to me. I couldn't wait to get back home to Connecticut. But I wasn't prepared for what I felt when I pulled into my driveway that afternoon. The safe, happy feeling that always filled me when I returned home after having been gone for a while was replaced with a profound sense of emptiness.

I dropped my bags in the kitchen and headed straight for my studio, my special place. I took out my sister's mass card, placed it on the fireplace mantle, and lit a candle next to it. "Teresa, I need to know something."

(I just looked at my clock right after I wrote, "Teresa I need to know something," and it's 11:11.)

"I need you to tell me who killed you. And for the safety of your children, I need to know now. But I'm kind of fucked-up right now, so I need you to tell Karen."

I shit you not when I tell you that my phone rang within five minutes. It was Frankie. "Annie, are you home?" "Just got here," I said. "I need to tell you what just happened." He sounded a little out of breath and excited. I could tell by the way he sounded that he was going to tell me something about Teresa. "Just tell me!" I said. "Okay," he said. "I asked Teresa to give me a sign to tell us who killed her."

I was all ears.

"I was at the beach just trying to chill and get my head together. I was talking to Teresa in my head, and I asked her to find a way to tell me who killed her. It just so happened that I was looking up at the sky. I saw Mark's name written in the clouds. "Annie, you know I have a hard time believing in this shit, but I swear to God, the letters *M* and *K* were huge and unmistakable, and it looked like the letters *a* and *r* in between."

Hmm. That's interesting.

"When I got into the car, I asked Teresa for confirmation, 'Tre, are you telling me that Mark had you killed?' I remembered how you told me you used the radio, so I turned it on and hit the scan button. I thought I heard the Beatles' 'In My Life,' so I stopped the scan. It was actually the very end of a different Beatles' song, but I felt like I was supposed to stop on that song, so I did and I asked Teresa, again, to give me confirmation that it was Mark. Then the next song started. It was 'Dirty Deeds Done Dirt Cheap!'" (The lyrics are about hiring a guy to kill your lady who is nagging at you night and day.)

"No way!"

"Yes!" Frankie yelled. "It was like she was trying to tell me what happened."

I couldn't believe Frankie—of all people—was getting these signs. Just a few weeks ago, he had been one of the biggest skeptics I knew, and now he was telling me our dead sister was trying to tell us that Mark had hired someone to kill her.

In between my shouts of *holy shit* and *oh my God,* Frankie continued.

"Wait, Annie, I'm not even done yet! Right after I heard that song, I was sitting at a stoplight just sort of looking around outside. I saw a store called Mitchell's Hardware. On the window, there were like these stencils of lawnmowers, rakes, shovels, and all kinds of stuff you would find in a hardware store. And smack in the middle was a stencil of an enormous hammer with the letter *M* on it."

I felt like I was coming out of my skin.

"Frank!" I shrieked. "Five minutes before you called, I asked Teresa too. But I asked her to go tell Karen, because I'm so freaked out."

"What are we going to do?" Frankie was freaked out too.

Simultaneously mystified and terrified, my thoughts immediately went to Teresa's kids. What would Mark do if he knew the police were onto him? Or that we were onto him? He had access to enough prescription drugs that he could make the kids a nice smoothie and check out with both of them.

No one was going to take Mark's kids away from him.

I hung up the phone with Frankie and sat in the silence of my kitchen.

You would think that after such extraordinary communication from my dead sister, I would be satisfied, but denial is truly incredible. I just didn't want it to be true.

"Tre," I said aloud to the empty room. "I don't know how you did that, but oh my God! Thank you, honey. Now don't get mad at me, but I *need to know for sure*. Maybe you could do that one more time? For the temporarily spiritually impaired?"

I could just hear her in my head, *"Are you fucking kidding me? I just drew his name in the clouds, told you in a song, and showed the murder weapon with his initial on it. What more do you want?"*

I paced around the kitchen for a minute and instinctively grabbed my phone to call Teresa and tell her what had just happened. My heart stopped. How many times would this happen? It just didn't feel like she was dead. The more she found ways to reach out from the other side, the more she felt alive to me. I wished I could talk to her.

I had to talk to someone. Karen. I'll call Karen, I thought. Just then, my kitchen door flew open, and Karen was standing there. She was pale and flustered. "What are you doing here? Aren't you supposed to be at work?"

"I got it," she proclaimed. "Got what?" I asked, even though I really wanted to blurt out what just happened to me ten minutes ago.

"Teresa gave me a sign, Annie, and it's unmistakable."

Oh my God! She did it again for me!

"Tell me! Tell me! What happened?" My heart was pounding.

Without moving from the doorway, Karen began, "Last night, before I went to bed, I did like you asked me to. I did a meditation to let go of any anger or fear so I could raise my vibration. Then I took Teresa's mass card, lit a candle next to it, and said, 'Okay, Teresa, I know it might be weird that I am asking you this, but Annie told me you would be okay with it. Annie needs you to tell me who killed you.' Then I lay in bed and did Reiki until I fell asleep."

I braced myself as Karen continued. "Just now, as I was driving home from work, I called my sister, Kelly, from the car. But Kelly didn't answer her phone, her husband did. So we made small talk for a while, and then I finally asked him where Kelly was. He said, 'I don't know. Why don't you call her?' I told him I just did. He said, 'No, you called me.' I told him, 'No I didn't. I called Kelly's cell phone.' And he told me again, 'No, you called my cell phone.' We went back and forth like this for a bit.

Finally, I said, practically yelling at him, 'I'm staring at my display, and it says "Sis." That's how I have Kelly's phone number saved. My brother-in-law finally got so fed up with me that he started yelling his name into the phone.

'Karen! It's me!

It's Mark! It's Mark!'"

It was time to call the detectives.

Chapter 35

The Alarm

Teresa was alive and kicking alright.

No wonder she chose that song. Her soul was unsettled, of course. Teresa was a mama bear, and she needed to protect her children. We'd seen what Mark was capable of already. If he could hire someone to bludgeon his wife to death, what else would he do? What if he found out the police were onto him? Would he kill himself and the kids? Would he kill me first if he found out that I had led the police to him? I was scared. But I had to do it.

Oh my God! My sister told me who murdered her, and now I had to call the detectives.

No, I did not tell the detectives that my dead sister told me who killed her.

But I did tell them that Mark had a motive. And I told them all the strange things that had happened since I'd arrived in Florida. The night Mark came to the hotel. The suspicious conversation he had with Daniele. Telling her to take care of the kids if anything happened to him. The insurance money. *The fake tears*.

And the alarm.

How could I forget about the alarm?

When I told my dad's sisters, Mary and Melissa, how and why I believed Mark killed my sister, their advice was emphatic. They told me to get a notebook, create a timeline, and write down everything I could remember leading up to the murder.

That's when I remembered the alarm.

It was the last day of our family vacation. Pack-up and clean-up was in full swing, with five families trying to leave an Airbnb by check-out time. My mother and I were in the kitchen separating food when Mark came in. He told us that his mother, who had been feeding the dogs while they were away, wasn't able to reset their home security system. Mark said rather than walk her through how to reset it, he told her not to set the alarm. I later learned from my brothers that he told them the same thing on the day we left. At the time, I didn't give it much thought because I was focused on packing and asking the kids to pick up here and there. There was a lot of commotion.

And that's *exactly* why Mark chose that precise moment to tell us about the alarm.

He wanted to plant the thought in our mind, but he didn't want us to react to it in real time. What he wanted was for each of us to remember the alarm wasn't set when Teresa walked into the house the night she was murdered. And he wanted all of us to be thinking the same thing: anyone could have gotten into the house.

And we did. It was the one thing we kept repeating over and over again in our minds, to each other and to anyone who asked us what happened that night. And it worked for a while.

I told the police everything.

They were already onto him.

Chapter 36

Dill

The night before my mother and I left Florida, I stopped in a 7-Eleven to grab some half-and-half. I paid for it, turned around to leave, and thought maybe I'd grab some wine for that night. I headed toward the wine, picked up a bottle of cabernet, studied it, and then put it back on the shelf. Why am I getting wine? I thought Everyone was gone, and my mother doesn't drink. I didn't want to drink alone, so I headed for the checkout.

Oh, the hell with it, I thought. Why would I not drink right now? I circled back to the wine, picked up the bottle of cabernet, took a few steps toward the checkout, and then turned around and placed the wine back on the shelf again. I must have repeated this scene about three times.

Alas, I arrived at the checkout without the wine and plopped my tiny pint of half-and-half on the counter. "One second," I said to the cashier, and then headed back to grab the wine. I felt ridiculous. I hoped nobody was watching this, but I was wrong.

As the cashier rang up my purchase, I glanced around my immediate surroundings and saw a cigarette lighter with a Dill pickle on it. Dill.

It was as if Teresa was watching me spin around like an idiot. I could hear her so clearly in my head as my eyes fixed on that pickle, "You're such a fucking Dill. Just get the fucking wine already!"

Honestly, who puts a dill pickle on a cigarette lighter anyway?

I knew Teresa was with me. Her humor was a much-needed salve. Since I got the dill pickle on the lighter joke, she kept it in her bag of tricks. A few months later, she used it again.

I was in Ocean State Job Lot with my cousin Robin, looking for some duct tape to fix a shelf in my freezer. I had never in my life repaired anything with duct tape, but I guess there's a first for everything.

If you've never been in an Ocean State Job Lot, they play great music. When I walked into the store, a sad mix of '70s ballads set off the waterworks for me. Okay, they play great sad songs too. I was a wreck during that time, and any sad song could have set me off. I walked around the store crying shamelessly. After looking around for a long time, I finally asked a clerk where they hid the duct tape. He told me where to go, and my cousin and I were on our way.

There was the duct tape, exactly where he'd said it would be. Robin and I spotted it at the same time. I laughed through my tears as Robin shrieked, "I don't believe it!" They had two types of duct tape. One was pink with flowers, and the other was gray with a repeating pattern of dill pickles and a tagline that read "Just Dill with it!" It was like Teresa was trying to get me out of my funk. I could just hear her saying, "There's no time for crying, Dill. You need to deal with this shit because we still have a long way to go."

That Teresa! As always, she was right. I had no idea how long and hard the road ahead would be.

(During the editing process, I found myself immersed in the scene, as often happens during the course of this writing. I thought to myself, that it had been a long time since Teresa has shown me a Dill pickle. The next day, Karen came over for a visit. Yes. That Karen. My wife

from another life that Teresa told who killed her. Mind you, I did not share my editing experience with her, and we haven't talked about my sister's Dill messages in years. "I brought you a little something," she said. She handed me a round yellow pin with a pickle on it that read, "I'm kind of a big Dill.")

Chapter 37

Looking for Signs

I was grateful that my employer encouraged me to take a leave of absence. I hadn't thought of it at first, but after a conversation with a representative from my company's human resource department, it was clear I had no other choice. My emotional state was fragile and I was simply incapable of working—and it wasn't just the grief.

It was fear.

I worried constantly about my sister's children, and I could barely keep it together. Every day that Teresa's husband managed to remain free was a nightmare. When were they going to arrest this guy?

When I wasn't spending time with my mother, I spent a lot of time with Karen. She took great care of me, cooking amazing meals, giving me massages, pouring wine, and pouring more wine. She supported me in any way she could and did her best to keep me grounded. Sometimes that meant taking my cell phone out of my hand because I'd been on the phone all day with reporters trying to figure out who Mark had hired to kill my sister.

I woke up very early one morning at Karen's house. I had gone to bed with my earbuds in so I could listen to my music. When I felt sleepy, I turned off the music, but kept the earbuds in to block out any background noise. A couple of hours later, I was jolted out of a sound sleep by, I kid you not, "Hammer Time" by MC Hammer blasting in my ears.

At first I couldn't figure out why Teresa chose that song to jolt me awake. She was the joke at all cost, but honestly. What I came to realize over time is that, from Teresa's perspective, all the world was a stage and she had just played her part. She was simply trying to bring some levity to an extremely unimaginable situation, and she did.

I got out of bed and grabbed my laptop, which I had with me at all times.

The murder investigation had led detectives to Mark's home state of Missouri, and I wanted to know why. Mark was from Missouri, and his best friend, Curtis Wayne Wright, still lived there. Could Wayne have driven from Missouri to Florida and back again and then shown up again two days after the murder? Was that possible? He certainly looked exhausted when I welcomed him into my condo for dinner the night he arrived in Florida. And he did spent most of the night trying not to fall asleep on the sofa. "Thank you for being here for Mark and the kids," I said as I hugged Wayne tightly. I felt sorry for him somehow, imagining the emotional strength he would need to support his best friend through his unimaginable loss.

Two months later, Wayne's face was on every local news program in Florida. He wore a green anti-suicide smock and chains around his wrists and ankles. I remembered that hug with horror and nearly vomited.

Now I sat at Karen's kitchen table and opened my browser in search of maps of the United States, trying to calculate a route from Missouri to my sister's house. The whole time, I was asking my sister to help me out. I figured she could have information magically pop up on my computer or phone, since she had already proven to be quite skilled at getting messages to me.

I didn't know what I'd learn from looking at those maps. I just wanted to give Teresa an electronic invitation to show up. You know, create a vehicle for her. I clicked on different maps, looked at the topography of the Mississippi River. Maybe the killers took a boat. Maybe a boat rental place would show up with a Dill pickle on it. I don't know. I searched around aimlessly for an hour, but nothing strange happened.

By now Karen was up and making breakfast. I closed up my computer. I knew she wanted me to get my head out of the investigation. I needed to chill. We talked about going to the beach, the park, or The Rock Garden—a crystal boutique we both loved and often went to. We also had some personal errands we each needed to tend to. Before we could decide what to do first, I got a call from a reporter at the *Naples Daily News*—a reliable source who checked in with me occasionally to see how I was doing and what I knew about the case.

Karen could tell it was going to be a long conversation. She grabbed a piece of my notebook paper and scribbled a note for me to meet her at The Rock Garden when I finished my call.

After I hung up from the call, I jumped in my car to meet up with Karen. I was wired and tired, but the tidbits of information I had learned from the reporter revved my adrenaline and curiosity. I started firing out questions like a lunatic to my dead sister. "You told me it was Mark. Why can't you just tell me the rest? Who did it? We can solve this together. I turned the radio on to create a vehicle for her to use.

Then things got really weird.

It seemed like every song on the radio, billboard, license plate, and strip mall sign was bombarding me with messages. It was like she was talking at rapid speed and she wanted me to take shorthand. Every lyric and song title, every billboard and license plate felt like a personal message from my sister to me. I felt like I was going crazy.

"You're going too fast," I said to the empty car. "Can't we figure out a way to talk to each other?"

By the time I arrived at The Rock Garden, I was in a tailspin from Teresa's undecipherable cosmic bombardment. "What the hell was that?" I thought as I got out of my car. My head was spinning.

I spotted Karen's car immediately and sighed with relief. I had to tell her what had just happened. I wondered if maybe we should go sit on the green. Maybe if I closed my eyes and relaxed, I could ask Teresa for a redo, only slower this time.

But Teresa had a better idea.

As I got out of my car and walked toward The Rock Garden, I immediately noticed a large sign hanging on it: "Intuitive Readings Today with Cassidy."

Are you kidding me?

Teresa was five steps ahead of me as usual. The Rock Garden was one of many destinations Karen and I had contemplated going to, and the only one with an intuitive reader who could connect me with my sister. It was too incredible to think it was a coincidence, and besides, I don't believe in coincidences anyway.

Karen was on the other side of the glass door watching me read the sign as I walked in. She looked up at me wide-eyed as if to say, "You believe this shit?" We both knew we were in the right place at the right time, and we weren't even sure how we got there.

Karen knew I would want a reading and had already asked the store clerk if we could get an appointment. After a few moments, a thirty-something natural beauty with large dark eyes and long, dark, wavy hair arrived from the back of the store to meet us and introduced herself as Cassidy.

Karen jumped right in, "Can we have our appointment together?" Cassidy was taken aback and started to tell us that she doesn't normally do that, but then she looked at each of us and said, "You guys were sisters in another . . ." and then, "No! Not sisters. You guys were married in a past life." Karen and I locked eyes.

That was it. We were sold. And off to the back room we went.

We took our seats at a small table in a dimly lit room and glanced at each other excitedly. I had had readings in the past. Some were good, and some were just okay. But just like there are good doctors and not-so-good doctors, the same is true with mediums.

Cassidy proved to be amazing.

She described Karen and me as if she had known us forever. Her accuracy was uncanny. As she described our past-life marriage, with Karen as my wife, she could have been talking about our present-life friendship. The dynamics were the same. "You," she pointed at Karen. "You're the quiet one in the background supporting her." And then she pointed at me, "And you are the one in front. I see you in front of an audience. Everybody listens to you." She pointed back at Karen and said, "You are like that song. You are the wind beneath her wings."

Tears started to roll down our faces. Karen and I looked at each other with so much love and gratitude. "Wind Beneath My Wings" was, in fact, our song.

Cassidy was pointing at me now. "You. Oh my! You were somebody who everybody listened to. You were a leader of some kind. Think, big Annie. Like a Moses-type figure. You rallied people, and they listened to you. You were kind. You didn't place yourself above the people. You were side by side with everyone." Then she pointed at Karen again. "And you were the wife, at his side, silently supporting him and helping him on his mission."

Next, Cassidy told me that I was going to be studying quantum physics, which I knew very little about at the time.

Cassidy never asked one question to either of us, and we never said one word, not even a yes or no. She just talked non-stop with incredible accuracy and resonance.

When our time was up, I asked her if we could do another thirty minutes, and Cassidy said sure. I looked at Cassidy, and all I said was, "My sister was murdered three weeks ago. Go!"

Cassidy looked at me for a moment and then took a breath before she began, "Your sister said she told you who killed her."

Holy shit.

"She's been giving you signs." Karen and I looked at each other. "She told you because she says you needed to know who it was."

Oh my God! Keep going, I thought.

"She knows that you are trying to solve her case, but she says you need to let it go and leave it to the investigators." Then Cassidy picked up a book. "Your sister is showing me this book." I knew the book. Teresa and I had read it and talked about it all the time! It was *Sacred Contracts* by Caroline Myss. Slightly and somewhat impatiently, I told

Cassidy, "Yes. I've read the book, no need to explain. What else is my sister saying?" I didn't want to waste one precious minute.

"Your sister is says she had a sacred contract and she knew what she was getting herself into. They made agreements, and someone had to play the bad guy. We always need someone to show us contrast. We need to experience the dark and the light. Only the bad guy didn't have to go that far. He chose to. And that's on him."

All of that made sense to me. How many times had my sister said she couldn't break her sacred contract?

"When she got to the other side, your dad was the first one there. And when the rest of her soul family gathered to celebrate, it was high-fives all around."

I pictured it in my mind. My Dad in his three-piece navy suit, looking like a movie star, with his brothers and sister and my grandparents. Their big Tottenham smiles. How happy Teresa must have been to be reunited with all of them again. It was the best moment I'd had since my sister was killed. But it was over in a second.

Cassidy continued, and I'll never forget her words, "Your sister says *'Don't get me wrong, the ending was horrible.'* "

The image of my sister veiled in golden light high-fiving my father and his brothers was painfully eclipsed by images of a faceless man swinging a hammer to her head.

I held my breath, wondering what she would say next, praying she wouldn't tell me what happened and feeling guilty for not wanting to hear it.

Cassidy continued with my sisters message, and these were her exact words.

'*You know, sometimes someone drives you so crazy—they make you so nuts—that you just want to kill them. But instead, they kill you.*"

It was as if Teresa was sitting across the table from me. Those were her words. The irony was sadly unmistakable.

Mark drove Teresa crazy. Deliberately. His perfectly planned antics were designed to sabotage her goals and her sanity. He knew how to press every one of her buttons to make her look like an unstable tyrant, while he came off looking like an emasculated and abused victim. A classic narcissist! How many times had she called me in tears after one of his schemes? "My fucking husband is making me crazy! I'm gonna kill him!"

How many times? More than I could count.

Cassidy continued, "Your sister says she's tired, '*I need to chill. I'm going to my beach where the sky is yellow and the sun is blue.*'"

And that was the end of the session.

How could that woman have known of all that?

Exactly.

She didn't.

It was Teresa.

Chapter 38

Just Breathe

A couple of weeks after our extraordinary visit with Cassidy, Karen and I set out for our annual camping trip to Hammonasset State Park, a magnificent stretch of beach and campsites in Northeastern Connecticut. We'd been taking this trip for about ten years with our kids and eventually their girlfriends and boyfriends.

This trip was like no other though. Not only would it end up being our last, but the heaviness of my sister's murder weighed on all of us. I thought I'd have to cancel. I knew the beach was exactly what I needed, but I just didn't have the energy or mental capacity to pack for a camping trip. But since my cousin Robin had taken time off from work to be with me, she not only came along on the camping trip, but helped me organize everything.

It was perfect. My son was especially sweet, as were the other kids, ranging from fifteen to twenty-one, to their "Auntie" Annie. Karen and Robin did a lot of the heavy lifting and poured their love onto me. I cry as I remember how broken I was and how all that love pulled me through.

We'd just come back from the beach and finished our lunch on the second day. A couple of the kids were playing guitar and singing while Karen and Robin put food away and organized coolers. I sat by myself at one of the picnic tables, staring down at the old splintered wood and faded bits of graffiti. I felt myself going down. Slowly but surely, the sadness was suffocating me. Teresa had only been gone for about a month. What was it going to feel like in two years? In ten? Would the grief ever end?

I can tell you that right now as I write this, almost nine years after Teresa's murder, it never does. The longing is like a deep channel carved into your soul. The thing is, I don't tune into that channel. Honestly, I'm good. But in this moment, I am brought right back to that day at the picnic table, and the tears are pouring down.

I didn't want anyone to see me crying, so I got up quickly from the picnic table and headed toward the bathroom building and slipped around the back. I leaned against the outside of the structure and slid to the ground, resting my back against the cool brick. No one could see me. Feeling safe and anonymous, I began to cry. And just as I started to relax and let go, I was startled by music coming from my phone. My phone was locked and in my hand. I had exited all apps and screens before I left the picnic table. How was it that Anna Nalick was singing through my cell phone, "And breathe. Just breathe."

I knew how.

When we were in Florida, the expression, "Just breathe," had become our mantra. At any incomprehensible moment, or emotional melt-down, you'd almost always hear someone say, "Just breathe," either to herself or to the person they were holding in their arms. Strangely, we all reported hearing the song "Breathe" by Anna Nalick, even though it was released ten years earlier.

Every time that song came on it felt like Teresa was with us, repeating the mantra along with the rest of her family. "Just Breathe." That song brought us a lot of peace and helped us transition into a life without Teresa. If only for a moment, it was like she was still with us. It was that mantra that turned my brother Frankie from spiritual skeptic to believer.

Left-brained and extremely logical, if Frankie couldn't prove it, he wasn't buying it. If I shared one of my experiences talking to dead people with him, I was guaranteed the classic "cuckoo la-la" glance from him. But grief can do strange things to a skeptic.

It was a couple of days after the murder, and Frankie had gone out for a run and then stopped at my condo to join us for breakfast. "I gotta tell you what just happened," he said as he made his way in. "You know how we keep hearing that song 'Breathe'?" I nodded. "When I was on my run, I said to Teresa, 'Listen, you know I don't believe in any of this shit, but if you play that song "Breathe," I'll believe that you can hear me.'"

Frankie also added that he deliberately intended to trip Teresa up because he was listening to a rock station, and no way would a pop tune by Anna Nalick play on his rock station. And he was right. Immediately after he threw down the gauntlet, Teresa dialed up "Breathe" by Eddie Vedder instead.

There you go, little brother, believe in this shit now?

Now, as I sat on the ground staring at my cell phone, I knew Teresa had opened my music app and played the song for me. I was overwhelmed by her timing. But in the moment, it was too much, even for me. I felt as though I would fall to pieces, and I just couldn't allow that to happen. "Sorry, honey, I can't do this." I closed the app and headed back to the campsite.

In an effort to distract myself from my sadness, I decided to call in my thyroid prescription. No segue there. The thought just popped into my head, and I went with it.

I touched the phone number for the pharmacy, put the phone to my ear, and was immediately put in a hold queue to music.

Are you kidding me?

It was "Breathe" by Anna Nalick.

Her omnipresence astounded me. The second play of that song was as if she was saying, "See? No need to be sad. It's really me. I'm still here." Her supernatural abilities made that impossible not to believe. Teresa was everywhere on that camping trip. And I guess that's what inspired me to invite my mother down for the day.

Usually when I camp, I shut the world off, especially this particular year. The only exception to that rule was my mother. To this day, I call her every day, but back then, if I wasn't with her, I called her at least three times a day. "Hey, Mom, how are doing?" Being the incredibly strong and selfless mother that she is and not wanting to spoil my camping trip, she told me she was fine. But I could tell by her voice that she wasn't.

I told my mother how Teresa played the song "Breathe" twice for me. My mother never tired of hearing stories about Teresa's messages. Nor did my mother tire of telling me how many times she would catch the number 11. Mom was a bona fide believer that my sister was still around.

"Mom, why don't you come up and spend the day with us on the beach?" My mother, a Pisces like me, adored the ocean. But I didn't think she'd want to make the forty-five-minute drive or deal with the traffic on the interstate. Besides, I was with my camping posse and figured she wouldn't want to be around so many people. I was so glad I asked though. Her answer was immediate. "Yes! I'll come."

I told her to bring along a few things in case she wanted to spend the night. "Ann Marie, I'm not going to sleep on the ground," she said, half shrieking as she does whenever she gets excited. "Ma, just bring a few things. You could sleep on my cot."

My mother is a pistol, or as Teresa used to call her, a "pipperdoozer." Why did Teresa call her that? Because that's what my mother used to call Teresa. Those two were more alike than either of them wanted to admit. When I think of how I will never get to know my sister as an old woman, I only need to look at my mother. And there she is, no doubt.

I knew having my mother with me would change the dynamics a bit, but she needed me. And had she not come, she would have been sitting home alone. Her husband is a loving a man, but like a lot of men of his generation who are taught to keep a stiff upper lip and carry on, he just couldn't be there in the way she needed. But I knew I could. And Mom did too.

After three phone calls from her asking what she should bring, four more from the road, and another two to direct her to our campsite, my mother arrived. She looked adorable in her beach hat and bathing suit cover-up. I hugged her tightly and then followed her to her trunk to get her things. "I decided I'm going to stay the night," she said as she opened it and pointed to her overnight bag. She had a big smile on her face, and so did I. I couldn't believe my seventy-five-year-old mother, who was definitely not the outdoorsy type, was going to camp with me. We hugged each other again and wept, happy to be together and heartbroken at the same time.

As I cradled my tiny mother in my arms, I noticed a box of my sister's mass cards in her trunk. I stared at my sister's face and smiled. I could just hear her scolding me, "What were you thinking? You can't leave Mommy home alone like that!" I was about to answer her back in my head, but she didn't give me a chance. Out of nowhere, on the calmest summer day, a strong wind kicked up and sent those mass cards in the air. Like leaves on a windy autumn day, Teresa's beautiful face swirled around my mother and me. Without missing a beat, my mother looked up at me. "She's with us, Annie."

The saltwater and sun revived my mother's spirit, and she seemed lighter when she left the next morning. "I'll be back tomorrow, Mom." I leaned down and kissed her as she sat in her car. "We'll figure out something fun we can do together then, okay?" I told her. My mother nodded in agreement, and she was off.

Meanwhile, Karen and I were trying to imagine a beach where the sky was yellow and the sun was blue. The two of us were relaxing on a blanket with my cousin Robin on one of the several beautiful beaches on this property. We were still processing everything that had happened during our session with Cassidy, and Teresa's seemingly constant presence on our camping trip. Our conversation was suddenly interrupted by Jess, who was running toward our blanket breathlessly. "Auntie Annie! Auntie Annie! You have to see this!" The three of us got off the blanket and followed Jess.

"I was picking up these seashells that I collect," she began, holding out her handful to show us the tiny shimmery peach shells. "I was in this one spot where there was a bunch of them." I followed Jess back to the spot. "But then something told me to move to another area. So I did."

I followed Jess about ten feet away from where we were standing. "A shell just like the ones I was collecting was sitting on top of that pile, so I picked it up." She extended her other hand. In it was a tiny shimmery peach shell. "Now look here." Jess pointed to lines etched in the shell. I saw it immediately, "Tre." I took the shell in my hand to have a closer look. I tilted it around, and I noticed something else: "Look, my name is there too." Jess continued, "The thing is, I didn't need to leave the spot where I'd been looking, because there was a pile of these little shells there. But it was like something told me to go look over there. I passed the shell to Karen and Robin. We marveled at the monogrammed seashell. I looked up at the sky. "Nice artwork, Tre."

Jess had been very intrigued when Karen and I told her about our experience with Cassidy. And since Jess's birthday was a couple of days after we returned from our camping trip, I treated her to a session with Cassidy, who was still offering readings at The Rock Garden.

While Jess was in the back with Cassidy, I busied myself in the store admiring crystals and jewelry. I couldn't help but wonder if maybe Teresa would pop in on Jess's reading. When the hour was up, Jess came out. "How'd it go?" I asked, hoping Jess would have a message for me from Teresa. I listened intently as Jess recounted moments from the reading that validated Cassidy's intuitive abilities. "She told me things that were spot-on, things she really needed to hear." Jess seemed very pleased, and I was happy she got what she needed from the reading. But I was still hoping that she would say something about Teresa. I waited.

"At the end of the reading," Jess said, "I asked Cassidy if Teresa had a message for me. And after a second or two, she said, 'Hm, Teresa wants to know if you liked her artwork. Does that make sense to you?'"

Jess and I smiled at each other. It sure did.

Chapter 39

Heart of the Matter

I'm not going to get into all of the details about the arrests and the trials. Nor do I wish to have the names of the individuals who murdered my sister printed in this book. It's hard enough to use the name of Teresa's husband, and even harder to remind myself of her affiliation. This book is not about those three men. It's about my sister and me. Our relationship. Our mission. But for the sake of wrapping up what happened next, Teresa's husband was arrested on February 26, 2016, six months after his best friend and another hired accomplice were arrested in August 2015. All have been convicted. Teresa's husband is on death row.

I have loved going back in time, reliving the most incredible moments of my life with my sister and rediscovering the magic we experienced in our journey together. At times I became so immersed in those memories that I found myself grabbing my cell phone to call her. But the rest of it, the murder? I had to let it all go. And there was only one way to do that.

I had to forgive those three monsters for murdering my sister.

I know. I know! I hear you. If it were your sister, you would never forgive them. Yeah. I get it. But know there are consequences to that mindset. I read somewhere that withholding forgiveness and harboring anger is like burning down your house to get rid of rats. In the end, you lose.

As Cassidy predicted, I did go on to study quantum physics, and for that I do understand the vibrational effects of unreleased anger. Everything is energy. Everything—even the chair you're sitting on right now, or if you're like me, the bed you are lying in as you listen to me narrate this book. Both are just harmless inanimate objects. But emotional energy? That's the foundation of creation. We create from our emotional energy that is tied to our beliefs. Think of your emotions as the catalyst for manifestation. It's literally how we make shit happen.

When it comes to anger, that's an emotion you need to either transform or release. Otherwise, it will make a very unpleasant home in your body. This was the very heart of Teresa's message. She used to quote Don Henley in her presentations: "You keep carrying 'round that anger, it will eat you up inside, baby."

But the truth is, you hurt more than just yourself. Unreleased anger affects all of your interactions, even subtly. The saying is true, "Hurt people hurt people."

And it might play out like this, for example: Maybe you're on your way to the grocery store. And instead of just shrugging it off when someone runs the stop sign at the intersection, you start screaming at the person and flip them a bird as they drive past you. And they do the same to you. Your anger is further fueled, and Lord help the next person who cuts you off or is driving too slowly in front of you. You can't seem to lay on your horn loud enough in protest of all these idiots on the road. You finally get to the grocery store, and you are pretty amped up, or should I say amped down because your anger has lowered your vibration.

Of course, you're going to get the cart with the thumping wheel that won't turn. The store is out of the one thing you really needed on your list, and now you're waiting in a long line at the checkout line. By the time you get to the checkout, you're not really in any mood to make pleasantries. In fact, you snap at the cashier because your bread got squashed at the end of the conveyor belt. And then you snap at her again when she gives you the total, as if she had anything to do with inflation.

Your anger has affected everyone with whom you came in contact creating a rippling effect throughout the Universes.

That's why I forgave those three monsters. It was my vibrational responsibility to do it, not only for my well-being, but for yours.

Chapter 40

Grief

The day after Teresa's husband was arrested, my mother and I got on a plane and headed to Florida to be with Teresa's children, Jo and Carm. Other than a few visits during the holidays and summer, my mother didn't return home for over two and a half years. This was no easy task for my then seventy-six-year-old mother, but it was the only way the judge would give her guardianship.

No one in my family had been allowed to see or speak to my sister's kids for months. Mark kept them isolated, not allowing phone calls or visits from any of us. By the time my mother and I arrived in Florida, the kids barely spoke to my mother and refused to be in my company. Those poor kids. They didn't know what was going on. Their reality was dictated to suit their father's narrative, which was that police had planted evidence, and their mother's family was working with the investigators to ensure his arrest. I later learned that Mark, among many outrageous lies, told his children that I murdered my sister.

That's the level of evil we dealt with for many months.

I had only been back to work for a few weeks when I got a call from a close media contact telling me that Mark Sievers was going to be arrested within the hour. "Oh my God!" I shrieked from inside my cube, my voice breaking through the humming of computers. Friends and coworkers popped their heads up, some heading out of their cubes and into mine just as they had eight months before. "They're arresting Mark today," I said in a whispered scream. The moment was electric. I quickly bolted out of the office and headed home.

The media was insane. These folks had been following this case for eight months, stalking Sievers, and sticking microphones in his face any chance they had. All the while, they never once got a word out of Sievers's mouth. I mean, if that alone didn't make the guy look guilty. Now virtually every local news network in Southwest Florida had their cameras pointed at Mark Sievers in his orange jumpsuit with hands and feet in chains.

And the police? Oh, how they had waited for this moment! They had pretty much known from day one that Mark was the man who'd orchestrated the murder, but they needed to have every single duck in a row. "We only get one shot at this. And we aren't going to take that shot until we know there's no way out for him," an investigator had said to me long before the arrest. At last, they had their man.

Media were lined up outside the police building with all cameras fixed on the double glass doors where Mark Sievers would soon emerge. I sat at my kitchen table, eyes fixed on my computer screen, staring at his face behind the glass. When the doors opened, Mark was flanked by Detectives Lebit and Downs. The detectives wore a solemn look of victory as they paraded Mark down the stairs toward the police car that was waiting to escort Mark to county jail. Strangely, Mark didn't look scared or resigned. He looked smug and indignant, like he'd just been served a burnt steak and had words with a disagreeable restaurant manager.

Not this time, Mark. You're going down, baby.

The level of relief that came with Mark's arrest was extraordinary. I could almost feel the tension release in every cell of my body, although the stress had already taken its toll.

My new doctor said I was like a prize horse that had run one race after another until it collapsed on the ground. But because my immune system and adrenals were so torqued up with fear, they refused to let me rest. Together, they kicked that horse in the stomach and made it get up and run again and again. The analogy was so incredibly accurate. Somehow, I hadn't been able to cry for my own suffering, but when she substituted that horse in my place, I took pity on the poor creature until I realized it was me.

My already compromised thyroid had gone bonkers, and I was suffering from severe pain in the center of my chest.

That's what fear did to my body.

Now, with the arrest behind me, the kids safe, and the media becoming less of an intrusion, I was able to breathe and take care of myself.

No more horse races for me. It was time to recover. Little did I know that grief had been patiently waiting for me and wanted to make up for lost time.

I hadn't allowed for grief. Sure, I cried. I cried all the time. But I never allowed myself to go all the way there with it: to let my mind imagine and my heart feel the magnitude of my sister's loss, the domino effect it would have in every aspect of my life. I had been too busy imagining her last moments on earth, fearing for the children, and waiting for an arrest.

For months I had been a warrior on a mission to find justice for my sister and protect her children. I often went at it like a raging bull, plowing through anyone who would get in my way, including my mother and my brothers, who wanted me to clear every move I made with them first. I remember standing on top of my coffee table screaming inaudibly on the phone at my brother Patrick to make him understand how I couldn't possibly keep the family abreast of every conversation I had with investigators, the media, and the Department of Children and Families. Things weren't much better for my mother and me. At one point, we didn't speak for over a month.

There was simply no time for grief, although it incessantly tried to abduct me with mental snapshots of every possible future scenario of a life without my sister and the precious times we'd had together. It was impossible for me to go there; it still is. I knew I would have to deal with it at some point. But until then, I visualized putting each image in a box, closing the box, and placing it very high on a shelf. Plenty of time for that later, I'd say to myself. After he's arrested, I'll deal with it.

And now the time had come to lay down my armor and sword and surrender to my grief. It was time to open that box that I had stuffed with my pain. If I didn't, I knew it would eventually kill me.

Sometimes I'd do it when I was alone. Other times, I didn't have that luxury. My grief erupted during an energy healing session, Reiki, or even a massage. Violent anguish that had ravaged my body and my being exited through howls and screams that surprised and relieved me. There were times I was sure I would never again experience joy. But Teresa had other plans for me.

Of course she did.

Chapter 41

Gratitude

A couple of days ago, I found my cell phone from 2015. It was a treasure trove of memories. My heart was racing as I scrolled back in time. It was all there. Everything! Hearing "Aquarius" in My Sister's Place. Finding tickets to see Elizabeth Gilbert. Teresa's 11s. We must have texted each other over one hundred times a week.

"She's mine," I'd said once during an interview. I didn't mean it in a possessive way, but I couldn't seem to find the words to define what she was to me. She was everything. My sister. My child. My mother. My spouse. My best friend. My healer. My teacher. My soulmate. For so many years, all roads led to Teresa. She was virtually a part of everything I did, even if she wasn't directly a part of the equation. She weighed in on everything that was going on in my life. My hopes. My dreams.

Our mission.

It was six thirty in the morning, and I was sitting at my vanity, drinking my coffee. The last time I had done this ritual was June 29 the year before. I was taken by surprise by the trigger the moment created. Our long-standing morning "Dill sessions" over makeup and coffee were gone—the precious time that belonged to us and no one else.

It was like losing her all over again.

I stared at the picture of her that I kept on my vanity. "Well, Dill," I choked through tears, and scrolled through my phone, looking for my Pandora app, "This will have to do, won't it?"

By this time, Teresa and I had a communication system. I put my music app on, and I asked her to be there, creating a vehicle for Teresa to use to talk to me. And on this particular morning, I really needed to hear from her as I nervously prepared myself to return to work, the scene of my trauma. I tapped the icon, and she was right there.

"Just Breathe" by Ana Nalick played right on cue.

How did she do that?

How was she able to be there for me the moment I asked for her? Was it because we were deeply spiritually connected? Or was she so tapped into my consciousness that all I had to do was ask her for a sign and she delivered? How she actually dialed up the song didn't confound me as much for some reason. That was just energy affecting energy. I felt like Teresa was on standby, just waiting for me to reach out. And her immediate response was a message within itself, "Dill, I'm right here, just dial me up, girl."

"You really are with me, aren't you?" I asked the empty room as I sheepishly looked around and clicked the double arrows on my phone to advance to the next song.

"Yes, I am," Teresa answered with "Breathe Me" by Sia.

Is this really happening? I hit the Forward button again.

'Yes. It really, really is," she insisted with "Breathe In" by Frou Frou. I stared at the display in disbelief. "You're really with me, aren't you?"

I hit the Forward button. Not recognizing the song, I looked at the display.

"Breathe In" by Lucie Silvas.

Really?

We were "Dilling!"

Chapter 42

Fade into You

It always starts out the same. I hear a rumbling sound in my ears like when I was a kid swimming in the river at my dad's house. As I would bob up and down, the sound from above the water would change to a rumbling sound as my ears dipped below the surface. I'm not sure why this happens. Is it the sound of my brain changing frequency from alpha to theta? Or is it the sound of my spirit trying to leave my body and having a few false starts and dropping back in?

I'm not sure what causes the sound, but that's what happens whenever I have an out-of-body experience, OOBE.

It was only a few months after Teresa had passed. The rumbling in my ears was followed by the familiar experience of floating above my bed. Only this time, a thought came to me. Without a body and the limitations of the physical world, I thought maybe I could experience instant manifestation—like whatever I thought of would happen. So I called Teresa to me.

I floated around for a short time in my bedroom, looking back to see my husband below me fast asleep. And then she was there, behind me. Yet I could see her in front of me. I could feel her, too, physically. She was pressed against my back, holding my hands at my side in hers. She stayed there holding my hands for what seemed like a very long time, and all I could feel was love. After a while, I heard her say very loudly in my mind, "Ann, don't you know I'm loving you all the time?" And then it was over.

I awoke the next morning with the experience fresh in my mind. Her choice of words struck me. "Don't you know I'm loving you all the time?" Why did she say it like that? Why not, "I'll always love you?" And as quickly as I asked myself that question, I heard Teresa answer me in my mind. "Because I am with you all the time. Loving you all the time." And that made sense to me.

I closed my eyes and remembered how wonderful it felt to be suspended in the air with my sister behind me. That was interesting too. Why was she behind me? I didn't know the answer then, but now, as I write this, I immediately think of what a person says when they support you. "I've got your back," or, "I'm right behind you."

The experience was visceral. I could actually feel her body at my back and her hands in mine. I quickly grabbed my phone and opened the first music app I saw. Teresa was there immediately. A smile spread across my face as I heard the intro music. I knew the opening lyrics that Mazzy Starr was about to sing.

"I want to hold the hands inside you."

Wow! Teresa was loving me all the time.

Chapter 43

One Year Gone

I didn't mind going back to work as much as I thought I would. The structure seemed to keep me moving along well enough. It was great to see my workmates, several of whom were very close friends. Even coworkers with whom I wasn't especially close and others who I knew didn't like me at all expressed such love and compassion that they remain very dear to me to this day.

Life went on, as the saying goes. Somehow, I was managing without Teresa in the physical world with me. Her consistent and creative ways of reaching me from whatever dimension she was in offered great comfort to me.

As the one-year anniversary of her murder approached, I made a decision to take time off from work. I wanted to be very present during the hour of her death. I knew her energetic connection to that date could cause her energy to be very earthbound at that moment, the date of her traumatic exit from the physical plane. According to the coroner's report, Teresa died at 11:19 p.m. on June 28. I have no idea how the coroner came up with such a precise time, but more interesting was that Teresa's birthday was 11:19.

When the 28th of June rolled around, I spent the day reliving everything I could remember about Teresa's last weekend alive at the vacation house in New York. Normally, Teresa was the life of the party, commanding everyone's attention with her bigger-than-life personality. She'd take over the kitchen, planning out every meal we would have for the weekend, all ultra-healthy, yet absolutely delicious. Since she was filming a television series, there should have been a lot of great stories that would have had us on the floor with laughter.

But the weekend was nothing like that at all. It was like she was on the outside, watching everyone and just taking it all in, as if she knew on some level she would never see us again.

We did play some Scrabble, but even that was weird. She didn't seem to be paying attention to the game. She didn't even yell at me when I still hadn't taken my turn long after the sand in the hourglass expired. Instead, she sat twirling her hair with that look on her face. She was putting all the pieces together, and too many of them didn't fit.

Late Saturday afternoon, Teresa began to suffer from severe heartburn. It was so bad she had to go to her room and lie down. As dinnertime grew near, she still hadn't come down to the kitchen. That morning, she had started a pot of black beans and was planning on making her famous guacamole and quesaDillas, but she never came back to finish preparing dinner. I thought about finishing the meal for her, but I knew I wouldn't do it the way she wanted, and Lord knew I was not going to wake her up and ask her. But at 6:00 p.m., I decided I would go in and ask if it was okay if I finished up the dinner.

When I walked into the bedroom, I was surprised to see Teresa and Mark lying on the bed, each propped up by an elbow with their head cradled in their hand, studying a backgammon board. They were both subdued and quiet. It was very strange. The two of them almost never spent time alone. Even when I visited them, Teresa made Mark sleep in the guest room so we could be together every possible second. Now, here she was, playing this ancient game that dated back to 5000 BC instead of playing Scrabble with me or at least finishing her recipes in the kitchen together.

What were they thinking about with this metaphoric game board between them?

I asked Teresa what she wanted me to do about dinner, and she told me how to finish off the beans and gave me her recipe for her special guacamole, being sure to tell me to add the jalapeños that Mark had chopped early that day. And as I recalled this moment, I have a clear picture in my mind of him standing at the kitchen island. He had this strange look about him. It was like he was struggling to keep himself from smiling.

A couple of hours later, Teresa came downstairs to join the rest of us who were scattered about playing cards or piano. "That was the worst heartburn I have ever had in my life," she wearily announced as she entered the room and plopped herself in a chair at the kitchen table. "I thought I was going to die."

I decided to look up the emotional manifestation that causes heartburn. For every physical manifestation in the body, there is an emotional charge at the root. There are a couple of wonderful books that correlate illness with specific trapped emotions. Two that I often refer to are *The Emotion Code* by Dr. Bradley Nelson and *You Can Heal Your Life* by Louise Hay. If you scroll through the alphabetized chart of illnesses in Louis Hay's book, this is what it says for heartburn: "Fear. Fear. Fear. Clutching Fear." My sister's body was responding to fear, even if she herself wasn't conscious of what that fear was.

The following morning, Sunday, we were packing and putting the house back together before we left. I can still see my sister's beautiful legs as she headed up the stairs to get dressed. "Hey, Dill, you should come and check out the new makeup I just got." Teresa and I shared a passion for high-quality, clean cosmetics, and she always introduced me to new product lines that met her high standards. It was customary whenever we could to put our makeup on together. I really wanted to spend time with her, but I declined. I wanted to help gather the rest of the food that we had brought so she wouldn't have to deal with it later. I knew she had been exhausted lately, and I wanted her to relax while I took care of her.

How I wish I had followed her up those stairs.

My mom and I were in the kitchen separating food when Mark came in. That's when he told us about the alarms. And it should have been a red flag.

Mark was beyond phobic about security. And my sister? Phobic didn't begin to describe her. She used to set her security system during the middle of the day when she was at home. Security and safety were lifelong, paramount concerns for my sister, and anyone who knew her could tell you that.

And, of course, now I know that's why the only person Mark didn't tell about the deactivated alarm was my sister.

If Mark had told Teresa about the conversation he had with his mother, she NEVER would have walked into her house that night. I know that because years before, there was a situation when Teresa had to go home late at night. Instead of doing so, she had a friend pick her up, spent the night at the friend's house, and waited until the next day when it was light out before returning home.

I found out two years after her murder from one of her close friends that Teresa didn't want to go home alone that night either. She even tried to find someone to pick her up from the airport. "I don't want to walk into that house by myself. Nothing good ever happens to me when I'm alone like that," Teresa had said to her friend.

After everyone had their cars packed and the beautiful house we had rented was back together, it was time for pictures. Mom, as always, wanted a photo with her four children. I have an image of that last photo burned in my mind. We looked so happy: Mom with a smile I have never seen since.

After various groupings of families and grandchildren, it was time to say goodbye. I went down the line hugging my brothers and mom, and then I got to my sister for our customary limited-edition goodbye hug. I squeezed her more than usual, "Love you, Dill. So great to see you. I'll talk to you later," I said, and she said the same to me. Then I did something I had never done. I stepped back toward my sister, grabbed her, and hugged her fiercely, almost knocking her off her feet.

Like Teresa, I believe a part of me knew I would never see her on this earth again. "Dill, what the hell, man? What are you doing?" she asked, shocked but laughing as I squeezed her tightly to me. "I don't know. I just don't want to let you go." I remember how she looked at me when I pulled away, as if to say, "What's gotten into you? We don't do this, remember?"

I arrived home with Mick around 3:30 that Sunday afternoon. Petr had already left very early that morning for a trade show in Manhattan. It was just me and Mick. After unpacking the car and hauling in laundry baskets and coolers of food—you would have thought we were going away for a week instead of two nights—Mick and I decided to order a pizza from our favorite place.

When Mick returned with the pizza, he departed to his room, and I settled onto my couch and cued up a movie. I was just about to hit Play when my cell phone rang. I looked to see Teresa's beautiful face on my phone screen, so, of course, I answered.

"What the fuck are you doing?" she asked playfully. She was at the airport and had several hours before her flight would take off and was looking to hang out with me on the phone. But I had other plans that involved a pizza, a movie, and shutting my brain off. A weekend away with your family can do that to you. We only talked for a couple of minutes. I had asked her how things were with the kids because they had been uncharacteristically disobedient that weekend. Teresa had really laid into them on Saturday afternoon.

We had been playing Scrabble, and Teresa went inside to grab a bag of tortilla chips—one of her favorite snacks. But when she saw they were missing, she charged down to the lower-level family room and discovered that one of her kids had brought them downstairs to their bed the night before. Teresa was floored. The kids knew better than to do that, and Teresa scolded them severely. After verbally dressing down her children, Teresa returned to the Scrabble game. She didn't say anything for a long time. She was twirling her hair again.

In our brief conversation that Sunday evening from the airport, Teresa told me that she had a very serious conversation with her kids before she left. From what she shared with me, those kids received a serious Tottenizing. At one point, she said to them, "I'm going to be dead someday, and I need to know that you'll remember everything I've taught you." I listened intently, never giving a second thought to her prophetic words. I didn't take her up on her tempting invitation for a two-hour Dill session, and she didn't give me a hard time about it. We said good night and agreed that we would talk in the morning, as usual.

I have replayed that phone conversation in my mind countless times. How differently things might have gone down if I had only taken that golden opportunity to have a long, uninterrupted conversation with my sister. I believe she would have shared what it was she was trying to figure out all weekend. And I know. I *know*! I am absolutely positive that at some point in our conversation, I would have most definitely, without a doubt, have said, "Oh my God, I can't believe you're going into your house tonight without your alarm set."

What would have happened if I had told her? Would she have called Mark and screamed at him and told him to get someone over to the house to set the alarm? Maybe. Or maybe that last piece of the puzzle would have clicked into place and the warning bells would have gone off.

I've played these scenarios out in my mind numerous times and have tried not to torture myself over them. I believe that if Mark's first plan to kill my sister didn't succeed that night, he would have found another way to kill her. In fact, court testimony later revealed that Mark had suggested that Teresa be killed at her office.

In the end, I don't believe Teresa could have escaped her fate.

I have no idea why one year later, I wasn't sitting in my studio with a lit candle staring at my sister's picture, or meditating, or doing something other than standing at my kitchen sink. I took a step backward to look up at the clock that was hanging above me. It was 11:00 p.m. One year ago at that time, my sister was being murdered. "Oh my God!" I thought. "What am I doing? I need to be still now." I grabbed a dish towel to dry my hands. I turned around to head to my study, but froze instead.

Teresa's mass card—that beautiful picture—was on the floor about three feet in front of me and one foot in front of my refrigerator, where it was previously hanging by a magnet. There was nobody in the kitchen. There wasn't a nearby breeze coming through a window to disturb it. There was only Teresa's electromagnetic field. She was with me.

She was loving me all the time.

Chapter 44

Air

One morning, a little more than a year after Teresa had passed, I was rummaging through my night table drawer to find my journal when I noticed the unopened set of Norm Shealy Bliss Oils that Teresa had given me. "Maybe I should start using these," I thought, thinking that maybe they would keep away the blues that February had faithfully brought to me.

The Shealy Bliss Oils contain five oils (fire, earth, water, crystal, and air) specifically formulated to assist the body in healing from a range of diseases and conditions, as well as activate spiritual awareness. You can use all of the oils together, in specific combinations, or even individually, depending on your needs. Each day, I would apply all of the oils to various points on my body as directed. I loved the way they smelled, and they seemed to keep me in a good headspace.

I was in a hurry one day and didn't have time to use all the oils, so I decided I would just choose one, but I didn't know which one to use. I clearly remember standing outside of my studio when I posed that question to Teresa. Sometimes, I did that, just ask a question out loud and see if she would be there. I turned on one of my stations and hit the Play icon, and immediately, a song called "Air" that I'd never heard before began to play.

A couple of days later I was short on time again. I posed the same question to Teresa, half doing so because I was convinced that she could not possibly name an oil in a song again. I opened the app, and to my amazement, the song "Air" played immediately.

(I arrived for a visit with Teresa's daughter, Jo, who is currently in college. Before we went to bed, she mentioned the Norm Shealy Bliss Oil. I didn't even know she was using them and told her that was strange because I was just writing about them in the book before I left to see her. "Well," she said, "I only brought one of the oils with me, Air." Today would have been Teresa's fifty-fourth Birthday. Such lovely synchronicity.)

Chapter 45

A Tiny Spark

It had been over a year and half since Teresa was gone, and time seemed to have both dragged on and flown by at the same time. Somehow, I met all my obligations, did what I was supposed to do, and managed to do it okay. I even performed in a couple of local shows with my band. It was great to perform again, but there were no sparks. Life was like eating food without tasting it.

I longed for the joy and excitement I felt with Teresa, the incredible, synchronistic messages that were leading us to our mission. I thought about our weekend in Newark all the time. What was the mission? I had been asking myself that question almost from the moment my brother Frankie told me Teresa was dead, but my quest to uncover the mission got derailed in the fallout. It was a question that had lingered in the back of my mind. Now that question plagued me daily. I started thinking that it was time to open that door again, having full confidence that Teresa would find a way to guide me.

I was driving to work and talking to Teresa out loud, as I often did. "Tre, now that you're in another dimension and have access to more information, maybe you can tell me what the mission is?" I hit my music icon for an answer, and "Mad Mission" by Patty Griffin was blasting through my speakers. I froze. This particular time felt so much like the time my ex-husband's name appeared on my screen. It felt like she was right there, just waiting for me to pose that question.

I could hear her in my mind, "Finally! I thought you'd never ask! Enough with the grieving shit. The mission is on!" I could feel her intensity, borderline Tottenizing, but I didn't know where to start. I asked her, "Can you tell me what the mission is?" And back to back, Elton John sang, "Holy Moses" in the "Border Song," followed with "Moses" by Patti Griffin. Cassidy had mentioned Moses during my reading. I asked Teresa if these Moses songs were a message for me. Again, I hit the Forward button and was answered with a song by "Yes." I hit the Forward button again, and "A Message" displayed on my screen.

As much as I enjoyed our multi-dimensional banter, I couldn't understand why she couldn't just tell me what the mission was with the same clarity she had told me who murdered her. Instead, she would continue with a consistent playlist to nudge me along in that direction.

Then I began to notice a musical pattern developing. First, one of the "Breathe" songs would play, and maybe that would be followed up by "Fade Into You," which then might be followed up with "In My Life." This was Teresa's way of tapping me on the shoulder as if to say, "Hey, it's me." Once I acknowledged her or asked if she had a message for me, I'd hear songs about messages, Moses, and missions. It always went down that way: a song or two to announce herself and then a few more about a mission.

During this period of mission, Moses, and other cosmic communications from Teresa, I received an email invitation to attend a webinar on an Emotional Freedom Technique (EMT) referred to as Tapping. This technique stimulates acupressure points by pressuring, tapping, or rubbing while focusing on situations that represent personal fear or trauma. When I saw the email, my very first thought was to delete it. I had plenty of work-related webinars on my calendar that, like this one, took place during lunchtime, which meant I couldn't go to the gym if I wanted to attend.

Teresa told me about tapping about eighteen months back; she'd been using it with her patients as well as with herself. Since Tapping was directly associated with Teresa and I found it peculiar that the invitation appeared in my work email, it felt like I was supposed to attend. Maybe there was something in the webinar that would help me move forward, or a message from Teresa in there somewhere. I wasn't sure, but I felt compelled to go and trusted my intuition. I clicked the register button.

I focused on the webinar, expecting to see a glaring message about the mission from Teresa. I looked for a word or phrase that might pop up on the screen and give me a clue as to which direction I was to go in next, or at least some sort of confirmation that she had, in fact, been nudging me along with her music playlist. Maybe the narrator would be named Moses, or there would be a tagline about a mission in the presentation somewhere, but that never happened.

In fact, the entire time I was watching it, I found myself critiquing it. The information was poorly put together, and the graphics were fair. The narrator had an unpleasant voice and greatly lacked presentation skills. But most importantly, there was no genuine passion behind the material. It was like they just wanted you to "sign up, baby!"

Don't get me wrong, Tapping is an excellent, non-invasive, safe technique that anyone can do with no real training required. But the only insight I walked away with after watching that webinar was how much better I could have presented that information. And that thought created a glimmer of excitement that lifted from the months of sullenness I had been experiencing. The Tapping webinar awakened something within me, and a tiny spark of inspiration began to flicker.

I had an idea.

Teresa never got the chance to reach the masses and teach them about the connection between their emotions and healing. And I never followed up on my dream of connecting people with their spiritual nature. I wondered, though, if I had enough information to bring these components together. I knew it would be a powerful combination to help people recognize and embrace their personal power.

My excitement seemed to expand by the second. And one profound lesson I had learned along my spiritual journey was that when something excites you, you must follow it! So I did.

Quickly, an outline for a presentation began to write itself in my mind. I took notes. I made lists. I looked for venues. I began to research other non-invasive emotional healing modalities For the first time since Teresa had exited this plane eighteen months earlier, I was genuinely excited and inspired. I hadn't felt anything close to this feeling of purpose since Teresa and I realized we had a mission.

Since it was the Tapping webinar that had reignited my passion, I began my research there. A search led me to a Gary Craig, the originator of this EFT known as Tapping. I began to watch tutorials and bookmark web pages I thought would be helpful. One day during my research, a video popped up called "The Biology of Belief" by Bruce Lipton, PhD.

At first, the presentation was very technical. Dr. Lipton talked in great detail about cells, proteins, and amino acids. I thought to click off, but I remembered Teresa and I had written an article referencing Dr. Lipton's research, so I thought I was supposed to keep watching. So I did.

Ultimately, Dr. Lipton had been laying the groundwork for a very intriguing lecture about the power of the subconscious mind. I wasn't even sure how I ended up on this web page, but there I was, completely enthralled and mesmerized by this adorable, whirling dervish of a man who, unbeknownst to me, was about to change my life.

As the sign in Newark read, *what happened next changed everything!*

Chapter 46

The Power of the Subconscious

I've often pondered the symmetry and mystery of the wondrous human body. What a miracle it truly is. I read somewhere that the odds of a single cell coming into formation is so improbable, if not impossible, that it was comparable to winning the lottery every single day for two hundred years or something crazy like that. That's just one individual cell.

Imagine the miracle of cell colonies that communicate in harmony to form organs and beings. We cannot begin to understand the miraculous Beings we truly are. And yet our fantastic physicality made up of over fifty trillion cells is only the tiniest tip of the iceberg.

The rest of what and who we are is all energy. Spirit. Consciousness.

Subconsciousness.

You can think of your subconscious as an intangible microprocessor that records and remembers everything it sees, hears, smells, tastes, and feels between the ages of zero to seven. The subconscious started recording when we were in our mother's womb. It downloaded all of your mother's experiences before you even arrived. And those experiences are only the beginning of what will grow into an inventory of beliefs through which you will perceive your reality.

Then, once you get here, you have even more learning experiences. You learn that if you cry, your mother or father will pick you up. Feed

you. Change your diaper. Snuggle you. Coo over you. But unfortunately, there are many babies who learned that when they cry, nobody
comes to their aid. Their perception of reality is generally one of a lack
of self-worth, which generally leads to lack in all areas later in life.

Now, there are some really wonderful benefits to this recording
system, especially when you stop and think about how much we need
to learn between infancy and second grade. We have to learn to crawl,
walk, feed ourselves, and use the toilet. Not to mention that we have to
learn an entire language, how to read and write, add and subtract.
Your subconscious records those instructions. And because our brains
are in a super learning state called theta, which is similar to hypnosis,
we're able to absorb a lot of detail in a very short time. That's why this
is a great time to teach your child several languages and introduce
them to musical instruments, art, sports, and so much more. They can
absorb so much so fast, thus the expression, "Children are like
sponges."

Our well-meaning parents have a lot to teach us too. And a lot of it is
useful. Chew your food before you swallow. Look both ways before you
cross the street. Respect your elders. Pay attention in class. Be nice to
your sister. All of this is wonderful so far, right?

But what about the other stuff they teach us? The fears and inse-
curities they unintentionally pass on to us simply through our obser-
vation of their behavior. Or worse, the mean-spirited and disem-
powering comments, like, "You're no good. You'll never amount to
anything. You're a loser." I even know people who were affected by
their parents saying, "If you don't behave in this store, I'm going to
leave you here," and then pretending to leave the store. Can you say
abandonment issues?

Now stop, because I already know what you're thinking. That you're
all grown up now. You're an adult. You can rationalize your past.

Maybe you studied psychology, or you've been to therapy, and you understand the source of any "issues" your not-so-perfect childhood created in your adult life. That's terrific.

There's only one very big problem.

We spend 95 percent of our day operating from subconsciousness programs.

Yes. You read that correctly.

So it doesn't matter much that you consciously recognize why your life is not turning out the way you want, or that you consciously employ steps, set goals, go to seminars, read self-help books, see a therapist, or whatever else you might do to turn it into the life you do want. Because before you choose to either engage in or recoil from an experience, opportunity, or behavior, your subconscious remembers everything you've ever believed about those choices before you and makes decisions based on *that* information.

Now go back to that kid who feels unworthy. What kind of choices will appear for him? It doesn't matter if he has consciously "moved on." His subconscious lives in the present tense and remembers everything like it was yesterday.

Our subconscious beliefs determine the limits of what we can achieve in every area of our life, from health, wealth, relationships, and self-esteem, to what we believe about our multi-dimensional nature.

Dr. Lipton uses a perfect analogy for this, that I actually use with clients and in my presentations. Have you ever driven your car for a long period of time and suddenly realized you can't remember driving the last ten miles? That's because you no longer need to think about how to drive the car or where you're going because our subconscious remembers habits and instructions and simply repeats them.

In the same way, our subconscious pulls from the storehouse of beliefs it has accumulated to create instructions and directions that determine our behavior and well-being. It shapes whether or not we think we are beautiful, capable, confident, intelligent, lovable, or worthy. It chooses our friends, partners, careers, and level of abundance. It decides whether or not we are anxious and depressed or calm and happy.

And just like driving our car, we go through life on auto-pilot and have no idea how we arrived where we are in our lives. It seems like no matter how much discipline or motivation we muster up or how many affirmations we repeat, we can't break behaviors or patterns that prevent us from arriving where we want to be. We are stuck in the same pattern, without our conscious permission.

But wait, there's more.

In addition to those crucial early years, the subconscious records any and all emotionally charged experiences throughout our entire lifetime, whether you're 7, 17, or 107. This can be anything from being laughed at when you gave a presentation to your high school class to having your spouse leave you or witnessing a car accident

Or someone murdering your sister.

I sat at my computer with my mouth agape as I listened to Bruce exuding brilliance and passion in this epiphanic lecture. *My subconscious was calling the shots in my life without my conscious permission?*

Of course! It all made sense to me. But I still had one very important question for Bruce:

How do I change my subconscious beliefs?

Chapter 47

Me First

As I digested Bruce's research, I took a moment and reflected on my life. Behavior patterns and experiences began to reveal themselves. The names and places might have changed, but the dynamics were the same.

For years the word *commitment* terrified me. I couldn't even commit to meeting a friend for dinner. I'd either cancel or struggle not to. When I grew older and thought it might be nice to have some friends over for dinner or host a small party, it caused me so much anxiety to plan and execute it that by the time the date of the event arrived—if I hadn't already canceled—I was emotionally drained from the whole experience. My inability to commit and complete a task was rooted back to my stepfather.

I had a front-row seat to my stepfather's bipolar behavior and violent explosions, and so did my subconscious. These episodes were very upsetting for me, and in some cases traumatic. As a result, that anxiety derailed any tangible or intangible experience I was about to manifest. I felt powerless to make anything happen for me in my life. Maybe my subconscious was conditioned to believe there was no point in trying to do anything because I was never going to see it through to the end anyway.

It's no wonder it took me three attempts to get my bachelor's degree, and that I never finished the book that I was so excited about years before.

I thought a lot about my relationships with men. Did my male coworkers feel threatened by me the same way my stepfather was? Despite my best conscious efforts, was my subconscious blaring out vibrations that men don't treat me fairly or allow me to speak up, and do I continue to draw more men like my stepfather into my life? Yeah, probably.

What triggered my depression? In January 1969, when I was not quite six years old, my handsome Daddy went off to the other side of the country, married someone else, and started a new family. What did my subconscious have to store on the hard drive about that one? That I wasn't enough? I wasn't loved? I didn't matter?

Meanwhile, I was left alone with a broken-hearted mother who sank into a terrible depression. A mother who tried to hide her deep sadness from me, but was unable to hide from my subconscious. I downloaded her feelings just by virtue of being with her. Now, every January, my subconscious remembers it's time for me to be sad, and by the time February rolls around, I am officially depressed.

Anger was at the top of this negative heap of subconscious beliefs. It played out in the way I chose to defend myself, and sometimes even express myself. It played out in road rage, lack of patience, intolerance, and a judgmental nature.

I was able to see that my life was a printout of my subconscious beliefs. These beliefs were keeping me from breaking free from life-long patterns of self-defeat and self-sabotage, anger, self-loathing, and powerlessness. I had no choice in accumulating these beliefs, and I wanted them gone! I wanted to change them into beliefs that would allow me to become the person I wanted to be and live the life that I wanted and knew I deserved.

How could I possibly expect my sister to lead me on this huge mission to serve humanity if I didn't have my own shit together first? I had no idea how to change my subconscious programs.

Why did I even doubt for a second that Teresa would show me how?

Chapter 48

Motoring

I was in Florida giving my mother a much-needed break from the kids when Rob Williams popped up in a YouTube video. Rob was discussing a powerful and transformative modality he originated, called PSYCH-K®, in front of a large audience. He described PSYCH-K as a unique blend of tools from contemporary neuroscience, research, and ancient mind/body wisdom. Using kinesiology (muscle testing) and simple balancing techniques, PSYCH-K allows you to remove at the subconscious level self-limiting beliefs that no longer serve you and act as roadblocks to achieving your potential and living the life you want.

Immediately interested and wanting to know more, I did a search on PSYCH-K and found the website. The rest, as they say, is history.

On the home page of the PSYCH-K website, there was a video called "Welcome to The Evolution of Consciousness." From the moment the video started to play, I became overcome with emotion and covered with chills. A knowing settled within me. I saw something much bigger here than my own personal transformation, a gift that could awaken humanity to its authentic multi-dimensional nature. I saw that peace on earth was absolutely possible. Immediately, my thoughts went to my magical weekend in Newark with Teresa.

I knew the way to our mission was through the subconscious.

It was as though, for the last fifteen months, I had been lost in a dark cave and finally found my way out into the light. I reflected back to the day I got that webinar invite. I can distinctly remember how hopeless I felt that day. I just needed something to get me back online, to get my pilot light lit again. And in all honesty. I had no idea what that even looked like. I was so far away from the life I used to live. I remember just looking at that invite and feeling a flicker of my sister's passion for alternative healing. And, man, I was willing to do anything that reminded me of her, even attend a webinar. That tiny thrill encouraged me to take a conscious step to bring some light into my life. And the moment I was willing to flip on the light switch, or at least swat at it blindly in the dark, Teresa was on standby just waiting for me.

Now, sitting with my mother in Florida, not far from where my beautiful sister's life was so violently taken from her, I felt an excitement within me that I hadn't felt since our night in Newark together. I had found the answer to why everything in my life hadn't been working. THIS was it. I knew this was the mission.

I signed up for the first available workshop that would take place in five months, and then I hugged my mother tightly and wept in her arms. "What's the matter, Ann Marie?"

"It's Teresa, Mom. She's leading me to our mission."

A couple of days later, I was back in Connecticut. The moment my request to take time off from work was approved, I signed up for PSYCH-K training. The feeling of excitement was glorious, and all I wanted to do was share it with Teresa.

I headed out to my car to run some errands. Before I started the engine, I took a solemn inhale. "Dill, this is our mission, right?"

I turned the key in the ignition. I clicked the power button on the car radio, and she answered me immediately with a song Kelly Keagy wrote for Night Ranger. Interestingly, I caught the song at the very end. If you listen to it, you'll see why that precise moment of the song was so powerful. The lyrics my sister chose addressed me as a "sister" christian, and that "the time had come" and that "I was the only one."

Yeahhhhh! I was motoring!

Chapter 49

How to Eat an Elephant

I attended the PSYCH-K Basic Training Workshop in February 2017, and by the end of that year, I'd completed three more. In less than ten months' time, this former procrastinator and fearer of commitment opened an LLC; created a website, brochures, and a presentation; booked a venue for an educational talk; created advertising; and did anything else I needed to do to get out there and start talking about the power of the subconscious mind. I had persevered through every obstacle with a resolve and focus I never had in my life. And you know what?

It was easy.

The work I had done during my training had removed the subconscious beliefs that previously sabotaged my goals and dreams. Now I had the privilege of working with individuals in private sessions, hosting workshops in my home, and offering educational talks about the subconscious mind and the incredible transformation that PSYCH-K offered. I wasn't able to quit my day job yet, but I was *committed* to transforming myself into the person I wanted to be and living the life I wanted. I was also very clear on the bigger picture; I knew Teresa wanted me to share this incredible gift of personal power with the world.

So I kept on *motoring*!

I continued to identify traits about myself, situations I was unhappy with, and roadblocks that kept me stuck in the same pattern. And one by one, I used this simple PSYCH-K process to rewrite each self-limiting subconscious belief with a belief that I wanted instead. Some of the balances I started with were as follows:

I set goals, and I achieve them on time.
I am committed.
I love and respect myself.
I am good enough.
I speak my truth.
I am treated fairly.
I am calm and relaxed.
I am patient.
I am slow to anger, recognize it, and release it calmly and respectfully.
I am kind and curious when others criticize me.
I deserve the best that love and life have to offer.
I joyfully release the past and expect the best now and in the future.
I forgive myself and others for all of the wrongs done to me, and I take responsibility for my own life.
I understand and accept that the death of a person or a relationship is a natural part of the cycle of life.

These new beliefs had a profound effect on how I experienced reality. For one thing, no one in my circle could believe that I had accomplished so much in only ten months. Hell, I couldn't believe it. I had never accomplished so much in such a short time. The normal urge to quit or create excuses that would derail my goal simply didn't happen. By ridding my subconscious of beliefs that blocked me every time I set out to create or commit, I ended the cycle of self-sabotage.

I also noticed that I was much calmer and contemplative and less explosive and reactive. I forgave more easily. I chose to accept and respect other people's opinions instead of judging them harshly like I once did. I didn't feel the need to be right, a former cornerstone of my character. Conversations that once would become arguments were now discussions where I was genuinely open to the other person's perspective. I listened more.

Over time, I was able to experience life in a loving frequency that begot cooperation over competition, understanding over self-righteousness, curiosity and compassion over anger, inspiration over jealousy, forgiveness over resentment. I was no longer on a roller-coaster of emotions. I never got really low, and I was able to enjoy the highs without getting burnt out from them. My life became calmer, more peaceful. Eventually, and to my great surprise, I grew to be more joyful than I had ever been in my life. My sister was dead, and yet I was able to let go of the grief and enjoy life more fully than I had ever experienced.

The night of my first informational talk in October 2017, I was sitting at my vanity, getting ready and talking to Teresa. "I can't believe it! Am I really doing this? I mean, are *we* really doing this." I'm not sure how, but the weirdest thing happened. The wall in front of the vanity was covered with a huge mirror, and in front of it was a mirror on a stand that I used to apply my makeup. In the corner of the vanity to my right was a framed picture of Teresa. Somehow the positioning of the two mirrors created an interesting image in the standing mirror in front of me.

Teresa's face and mine were side by side, joined at our foreheads.

We were on this mission together.

Chapter 50

Vibe Matters

My mother used to tell me about vibrations. I didn't really understand too much of what she meant when I was a boy. It scared me, the word vibrations—*to think that invisible feelings existed. She also told me about dogs that would bark at some people, but wouldn't bark at others, and so it came to pass that we talked about good vibrations.*
—Brian Wilson, The Beach Boys

Intrinsically connected and separated only by form, we are vibrational beings affecting everything throughout many Universes. Everything we think, feel, or say carries a vibration out to the Universe, and in return, the Universe matches that vibration to manifest our experience. This is called the *law of attraction*, and it is how we create our reality in every moment.

It doesn't matter whether or not you believe in the law of attraction, just like it doesn't matter whether or not you believe in the law of gravity that is keeping this book in your hand or your earbuds in your ears.

If you let go of something you are holding in your hands, it will most definitely tumble downward and land on the closest available surface. Ba da bing, that's gravity. It's not something you ever have to think about. It simply is.

Here's what I urge you to understand: the law of attraction is every bit as absolute as the law of gravity.

And it kind of works like this.

Our emotions, which trigger thought, word, and deed, are like transmitters that send out a frequency, and in turn, the law of attraction finds a match for that vibration. If your emotions are fear-based emotions such as anger, hate, fear, envy, or lack, for example—and the list goes on—they have limited reach, meaning they can only match equally low-vibrating frequencies.

Think of it like this. Back in the '60s, television sets used antennas called *rabbit ears* that only had access to a few local stations. In a similar way, if you are holding fear-based emotions, aka low fre-quencies, you are equally limited in your access to the experiences you can bring into your life, and the ones you do have access to will match those fear-based emotions. It's like the grocery store scenario I talked about earlier. One negative experience begets another, and on it goes.

But when we are vibrating love-based emotions, we trade in those rabbit ears for a satellite that provides us with access to an endless number of stations that can only manifest into experiences that match that vibration. That's when we are literally in the flow. We feel more inspired and lighthearted. It seems like everything is going our way without any resistance.

When we are vibing love, joy, and happiness, we're able to deal with it from a place of love, release it, and then move on. So instead of flip-ping off a driver who ran a stop sign on the road, you might shrug it off or laugh. Instead of reacting to anger with anger, you might find that you are curious, compassionate, and forgiving.

Raising your vibration has other benefits. It gives you access to information in a place from which you don't have access at the conscious level. This is when we get information from higher realms. It's when we get that spark of inspiration to write a song, invent something, or solve a problem. Or to be at a certain place at a certain time. That's why Einstein said you can't solve a problem from the same place in which it was created. Einstein understood higher dimensions of reality.

I already know what you're thinking.

If this law of attraction is as absolute as the law of gravity, then why aren't your affirmations working? Why hasn't your vision board turned into reality for you? Right? You might even have sticky notes on your bathroom mirror and refrigerator as a constant reminder to repeat, "I love and accept myself," "I am peace," or, "Money flows to me easily and abundantly." Or maybe you have a vision board loaded with pictures of experiences you want to see in your life.

How are those working out?

Exactly!

Here's why. We spend 95 percent of our day in subconsciousness and only 5 percent of the day in consciousness. Remember?

Conscious thoughts are about wishes and desires, and your vision boards and affirmations are nothing more than that. Those wishes and desires can only manifest if your subconscious believes in those wishes and desires. There must be alignment between consciousness and subconsciousness. Why?

Because the law of attraction responds to subconscious vibrations.

So you can say, "Money flows to me easily and abundantly," all day long, but if you were raised believing money is the root of all evil or constantly heard your parents say they'll never have enough money, or watched them work four jobs between them and still not have enough money, then that's what your subconscious believes about money and abundance.

And that subconscious belief about money carries a vibration that the law of attraction absolutely responds to. So if you don't change your subconscious beliefs about money, you will continue to sabotage your wishes and desires no matter how many times you write them down or visualize them.

Think of it like this: Imagine you are listening to loud music through your earbuds, and at the same time someone is trying to talk to you. Obviously, you can't hear what they're saying because you're listening to the music blasting through your earbuds.

Now imagine you are the Universe, the music coming through the earbuds is your subconscious beliefs, and the person talking to you is your conscious affirmations.

In the same way you cannot hear the person talking to you, the Universe cannot offer conscious affirmations about money. It is completely overpowered by your subconscious, and that is blasting what you *actually* believe about money 95 percent of the day.

Here's the great news: if you don't like what your subconscious creates for you, you can change it.

We are not victims of circumstance, but truly creators of our reality. This is, without question, fundamentally the most important thing we need to know about being human on this planet.

We've had this creative power all along.

And that's why accessing the subconscious is critical to our mission.

Chapter 51

Irish Intuition

I always wonder what my life would be like if Teresa were still alive, here in the physical world. How all of this would have played out for her. For me. The kids.

A few months before I discovered Bruce Lipton and Rob Williams's PSYCH-K, I was renting a beautiful Airbnb on Lake Champlain on Isle La Mott. The lovely Irish woman who rented the space to us lived on the property as well. I had no idea she would be around during my stay. Not only did this woman hold two PhDs, but she was also an incredible intuitive.

During an unsolicited reading, she told me that my sister sacrificed her life for her children, not consciously, of course. I had never looked at it that way before, but believed she was probably right.

Mark had isolated my sister's children from the world, from reality, actually, and turned them against everyone who was not in line with his narrative. He controlled who they talked to, where they went, and what they did. And obviously, he was capable of murder. If Sievers were rocking in the free world instead of a dead man walking, that sociopath would have ruined those beautiful little souls.

The woman also told me Teresa and I were Indian brothers in a past life that had later become passionate rivals. That, she explained, was why we had such resistance about showing each other physical affection.

"Your sister says that you will be continuing with her work." The woman's accuracy had been pretty compelling up until that point, but now I was confused. "I don't think so," I said to the woman. "My sister was a doctor. I'm not seeing a segue here." The woman laughed and then said very matter-of-factly, "No, you're not going to be a doctor. That's not what she means. But you will continue doing her work." At the time, that didn't make any sense to me at all. I was still in the early stages of grief and consumed with worry for my sister's kids and constant prayers that Sievers would never see the light of day.

A couple of years later, that lovely Irish woman reached out to me for a PSYCH-K session. After the session, we chatted for a while, and I reminded her what she had told me four years earlier. "You were right," I told her. "I am continuing my sister's work. Right where she left off."

Chapter 52

The Missing Piece

"If I could just get out of this body, I could get so much more shit done!" Honestly, who says that? My sister did. She said it to one of her patients, who later shared it with my family at Teresa's memorial service. I can't think about Teresa saying that without immediately hearing my mother shriek, "That Teresa!" It was classic, no-filter Teresa. To hell with decorum. Teresa brought authenticity to new heights. The problem was patience. My sister didn't have any, *not even on a good day*.

In 2015, although she was spending much energy considering the fallout that would ensue if she left her marriage, she was consumed to the point of exhaustion with her vision to reach the masses with a new healing paradigm. It was like some part of her knew that she didn't have that much time left on this planet and couldn't seem to work hard enough or fast enough. She was almost there, but only now can I see that she was missing something. That something was why my sister was telling the Irish woman that I was going to continue her work.

That something was the word *subconscious*.

A few years ago, I was watching an episode from Teresa's television show that never aired. She looked directly into the camera and said something like, "I can't make you well. Only you can heal yourself." No mention of the subconscious though.

Shortly after that episode was shot, and a few months before she was murdered, Teresa gave a talk, and the key takeaway point was the relationship between stress and disease. Yet, once again, she never talked about the subconscious. She pointed to emotions—often referring to them as stress—as the root cause of illness, but she never referred to the subconscious.

It was also around this time that I wrote an article for my sister that referenced Bruce Lipton's research on epigenetics, or emotions above genetics. Again, that was the reason I watched the "Biology of Belief" video that popped up after attending the Tapping webinar. I remembered our article about Bruce. But, again, the subconscious was not discussed in the article. Now, as I looked back, I couldn't understand how she could discuss Dr. Bruce Lipton and the relationship between emotions and disease without mentioning the word subconscious.

I did a little research.

I found an article by Dr. Lipton written in the May/June 2014 issue of *Resurgence and Ecologist*, which was right around the time Teresa had started discussing epigenetics. In Dr. Lipton's article, the subconscious isn't introduced until after going deeply into his research. I'm guessing my sister got bogged down in Petrie dishes and stem cells and saw the definition for epigenetics—emotions over genetics—and never finished reading the rest of Dr. Lipton's article.

Teresa was on the cusp of putting it all together, yet I now realize identifying the subconsciousness as the key to reconciling stress was a critical omission on her part.

If Teresa had come upon the "Biology of Belief" video on YouTube like I did, or read the book, I can only imagine what her excitement would have been like. I am sure, like me, the moment she understood that the subconscious was not only the key to our health, but literally the launching pad to creating our physical reality and the access point to our spiritual nature, she would have felt like she had found the holy grail. Like me, she would have been screaming at her computer screen, albeit more aggressively, "Alright already, Bruce! I get it! So how do I stop my subconscious from fucking up my shit?"

After screaming at Bruce, she would have calmed down—only a little—and researched modalities to rewrite the subconscious. She would have called me up, cracking her whip and insisting that we find the best modality to rewrite the subconscious. She probably would have signed us both up for PSYCH-K training while at the same time doing a property search so I could move to Florida and work for her—something she was always trying to make happen.

That's how Teresa rolled.

I would have been scared to make the move and concerned about logistics, and she would have told me to shut up and trust her. In the end, I would have listened to my little-big sister because that Teresa never steered me wrong.

We would have been flying high the way we were that weekend in Newark because we would have figured it out. She would have said to me exactly what I said to her that night I saw our two faces reflected in my makeup mirror. Only she wouldn't have asked me. She would have proclaimed it as law: "Dill, this is it! This is our mission. Now quit your stupid, fucking job and get your sorry ass down to Florida and let's do this!"

Chapter 53

Departures

There's nothing like Florida in February, especially if you grew up in the Northeast. Don't get me wrong, I adore the snow and love to snuggle in when a winter storm hits. And I love the four seasons. There. I said it. It's not just a comeback line I say to Floridians when they tease me with complaints of sixty-five-degree weather, knowing I'm freezing my ass off at twenty degrees. I am a New Englander through and through, and I'll take the good with the bad. But, man, do I love Florida in February.

I had long dreamed of moving to Florida to be with Teresa. We both used to fantasize about how great it would be to see each other every day. It was understood that we would live next door, across the street, or—at the furthest—around the block from each other. "Can you imagine how cool it would be knowing that we could just pop in and see each other whenever we wanted?" I'd say to her.

We talked about having coffee together on weekend mornings. Taking turns making dinners. Running errands for each other. And best of all, we could really get to know each other's kids. That was the best part for Teresa because there wasn't anybody around to stay with the kids if she wanted to get away for a bit. I might not have been a fan of watching other people's children, but when it came to my sister's two, I welcomed any time to spend with them. These two were the most brilliant, entertaining, funny, preciously sweet kids I'd ever known. I loved being with them, and they loved their Auntie Annie.

Unless it was completely impossible for her, Teresa always made time to pick me up at the airport when I visited her in Florida. The queen of time management, if she could save five minutes here and ten minutes there, she was doing it.

So I had to text her "the second I landed," as she insisted.

One time my phone volume was off, and I didn't see that she'd texted me to say she would be waiting for me at departures to avoid the long line in arrivals. So unwittingly, I grabbed my luggage and stepped out to the curb at arrivals, scanning down the long line of cars looking for her Mercedes-Benz 4MATIC®, her "doctor car" that I mercilessly broke her balls about.

I couldn't see her anywhere, but I didn't bother to call and ask where she. It would only annoy her if I tried to undermine her time-management skills.

Little did I know that my volume was down, so I hadn't seen several, "Where the fuck are you?" and, "Pick up your goddamn phone," texts, along with five missed calls from her. I was afraid to call her and tell her that I was at Arrivals, so I texted her instead. I waited for her to call me back and unleash her wrath upon me. But to my surprise, she didn't text or call back.

A few moments later, off in the distance, I heard the clomping of high heels hitting the pavement hard. I turned my head in that direction to see my sister about one hundred feet away, power walking up the sidewalk, dressed to the nines in her big sunglasses, and hot-roller curls bouncing. I thought for sure she would start screaming at me. Instead, she just yelled in her loudest voice, "You're an absolute Dill!" and then started laughing, running toward me with her arms wide open, not giving the slightest shit what anyone thought.

Chapter 54

Rescue Mission

It was February 2018, and I was waiting outside to get picked up at Southwest Florida International Airport. Only my sister wasn't waiting for me. I wouldn't see her making her way toward me like a flamboyant rock star laughing or screaming at me. Teresa had been gone for two and half years already.

Now, I waited for my seventy-eight-year-old mother to take me to the condo I had rented in Coconut Point in the same complex where she was now raising my sister's two kids. After two years on her own, she was finally getting a break, as I was finally able to make arrangements, if only for three months, to work remotely so I could help my poor, tired mother. She never complained, but my brothers and I knew she was struggling with the kids. Good friends of my sister, Donna and Joe, who are now family to me and also lived at Coconut Point, used to help out my mom whenever they could. They had front-row seats to the shit show that was unfolding down South and kept me informed.

Aside from the kids' unimaginable trauma, their minds had been so twisted by Mark. He had told them the police had planted evidence and that my family was responsible for their father's incarceration. They were told to trust him and no one else, especially me. Mark knew I was the driving force working with investigators, and he made sure the kids knew that.

Incredibly, Mark was allowed to call those kids all day long from jail—often ten times a day—drilling them with questions, reinforcing his mandate to mistrust, laughing at and encouraging their pranks and feistiness. Mark also recruited his family, particularly his mother, who lived only a few minutes from the children, to reinforce his dictates, and continued to provide Mark with access to the kids long after the court finally put a stop to unsupervised phone calls. For almost three years, those innocent children believed that I and my family were the enemy.

Something had to be done. Someone had to step in to help Mom. Since I was the only one who had the flexibility to work remotely, it was me. Unfortunately, I was only allowed three months of remote working. So from February 2018 to May 2018, my home was sunny Florida.

I couldn't believe how much my mother had aged. She had been running on pure adrenaline for almost three years. My sister had only been dead eight months when my mother left everything to raise the kids. She didn't even have time to grieve. To top it off, she had no time to recover from the fear and anxiety we all felt leading up to the arrest. When I arrived to take over, the adrenaline that had kept my mother alive and her grief at bay seemed to run dry.

I popped over to her condo one afternoon while the kids were at school. I saw something I'd never seen. This woman, my mother, who wouldn't even take a break from doing laundry or mopping the kitchen floor on a Friday night to watch *The Partridge Family* with her kids, was lying on the couch in the middle of the day watching *Family Feud*. This was not the mother I remembered. Watching television during the day was a misdemeanor.

My mother was toast.

It took some time, but after a while, my relationship with the kids was on the mend. In the two years that my mom was solo in Florida, I had been down to visit a half dozen times. At first, I had to stay at a hotel or rent an Airbnb because those poor kids were afraid to let me stay with them. I could only visit my mother when they were in school or if they were at Mark's mother's on the weekend.

Gently and with persistence and consistence, I was able to rekindle their love and trust for their Auntie Annie. The fun aunt. The mysterious aunt who would burn sage in their rooms to ensure sweet dreams. The theatrical aunt who would reprise her role as Fastrada from *Pippin* and other shows they hadn't been able to attend. The aunt who dressed them up in costumes and makeup for their pretend games. The aunt who they knew deep down in their subconscious minds loved them fiercely. It was slow and steady, but they started to come around. They began to welcome the levity I brought to their lives with their grandmother, who had done all she could do to keep her head above water. I was making inroads, building their trust a teeny tiny bit at a time.

At the same time, a huge win in court that mandated supervised calls between Mark and the kids, and no more than one time per day, was monumental to our healing. Mark was forced to follow strict guidelines for appropriate conversations. Namely he could not speak of the murder case in any context or recall memories about my sister from his select repertoire that depicted only the moments when my sister lost her temper. He wasn't allowed to speak my sister's name, or anyone's name from Teresa's family. The moment he broke those rules, he was told the call would be terminated.

But, man! That son of a bitch thought he was so slick. He always found his way around rules. He tried anything to maintain his influence over the kids. He'd reference songs, movies, books, Bible verses—devise any code he could—to continue his brainwashing.

Luckily, my sister's close friend Kathy volunteered to monitor all the phone calls and was unanimously accepted by my family. Nothing got by her. Even the time he just so happened to mention to the kids a "really good book he was reading," which Kathy immediately Googled. The book was about a man wrongly accused of killing his wife, when in fact it was her own family who murdered her to inherit her money. Kathy had this monster's number. She knew what he was capable of, was always five steps ahead of him, and took great pleasure in reprimanding him and terminating phone calls.

Buh bye, Markie. Go away. You have no power here.

Now that Sievers was smacked down into place and the kids began doing their own research on the case, I was able to get closer to them and have conversations with them that were long overdue. They were smart. They understood that their grandmother was too old to take care of them indefinitely and that she needed to get back home with her husband. They knew I couldn't remain in Florida. They were crystal clear on the unforgiving logistics their grandmother and I endured. I tried to offer a way out for them. Did they want to stay in their tiny, cramped condo with old, tired Mimi, or might they imagine living with fun Auntie Annie and Uncle Petr? Having their cousins around them?

No. They wanted to stay in Florida. End of discussion.

It was April, and in two months, my mother was scheduled to go before a judge to ask if she could please, please, pretty please take her deceased daughter's children back to Connecticut with her so she could be with her aging husband, who had now been living alone for over two years. Now, I knew this would be futile. She had already stood before the same judge a year earlier, and he had previously denied my mother's petition. His reasoning? The kids want to stay in Florida, and that's where they're gonna stay, Grandma.

My broken mother was stuck in Florida with two broken children who refused to leave. All I wanted to do was take my mother and those kids and get the hell out of there. The clock was running out for me. I only had one month left with permission to work remotely, and then I would be forced to return to Connecticut by May first. How could I possibly leave my mother? I felt if I left her, she would see an early grave. We were at the mercy of the courts and my boss.

Or were we?

Chapter 55

Exit Plan

The warmth of the Florida sun did nothing to assuage my sullenness. I felt like I was the one in prison.

It was a Sunday in mid-April, and I was sitting by the pool drinking my morning coffee. I was exhausted and defeated. Soon, I would be leaving my mother in Florida to raise the kids by herself indefinitely.

I knew working with my subconscious would release the resistance I was feeling and allow me to align my vibes with what I wanted to create instead of the miserable situation I was in. But I was so distressed that I couldn't get an accurate muscle test, which is heavily relied upon when using PSYCH-K. I felt powerless. I thought about reaching out to another PSYCH-K facilitator to do a session with me, but I didn't have the energy to even do that. So I sat there drinking my coffee and crying. My vibes were circling the drain. I was going down.

Then something happened.

This time, it was different. It wasn't a voice in my head. It was a magical burst of inspiration that sprang from my infertile imagination, a Divine download, an instantaneous and absolute knowing. I snapped from self-pity to self-empowerment from one minute to the next with a fool-proof exit plan to get us all the hell out of Florida.

If I couldn't convince the kids with pure logic that we had to get out of Florida, I was going to win them over with materialism, damn it! I ran back to my condo, opened my computer, and started searching for a big, beautiful house in Connecticut that would knock the socks off those kids.

I knew exactly what to look for.

It had to have a built-in swimming pool so they could splash around and have relay races with their cousins, a huge game room where they could invite their new friends over to play ping-pong and watch movies. A fireplace where they could drink hot chocolate while discovering the beauty of snowfall. Lots of land with varied species of trees to surprise them with rich colors each fall. Beautiful bedrooms filled with sunshine and decorated in their personal style. I was going to buy the most incredible house those kids had ever seen. It was going to be so amazing, they'd spring from that cramped 750-sq.-foot condo in Florida and jump straight into that swimming pool.

Chapter 56

Instant Manifestation

The search criteria was narrow. The timing was tight. I needed to manifest a very specific house and move into it in a very, very short time. And to narrow things down further, it needed to be within a short driving distance from my mother. Since she was the legal guardian, Mom would have to move in with us, too, which not only required yet another bedroom, but quick access to her home where her husband had been living alone.

The real challenge was timing. It was almost the end of April, and I had to be moved in before the kids met with the judge in the last week of June. This house was required to blow their doors off so they could tell that judge—no, demand—that they wanted move to Connecticut. If their doors stayed intact, I was going to be stuck with a monstrous, empty house.

Another huge hurdle arose among the few houses that did meet my long list of criteria. They were home to children with parents who, understandably, didn't want to close on their property until after the school year wrapped up at the end of June. So even if we were lucky enough to find the right house, we wouldn't be able to close until after the court date, and that was pointless.

With so many odds stacked against this seemingly impossible feat, the naysayers in my family grew concerned about the financial risk. What the hell was I going to do if I actually found this pie-in-the-sky homestead and the kids still refused to come to Connecticut?

I wouldn't back down though. I believed it would all work the moment the idea had been downloaded. I knew my sister, in her multi dimensional wonder had devised this plan from another place—a place where three-dimensional impossibilities didn't exist, where any man-made roadblock perceived or imagined would disintegrate into sawdust, where miracles were created and delivered to reality.

Two months after my Divine download, I, along with my mother, Teresa's kids, my husband, my son, and three cats, moved into that dream house, complete with all the bells and whistles and less than two miles from my mother's house. How?

Because, dead or alive, that Teresa could get more shit done than anybody.

Chapter 57

Grammy's Day

June 8 was a significant date for Teresa and me. It was the day our beloved Grammy left this world. On that day, my grandmother had been lying on her deathbed unresponsive for hours. But to everyone's amazement, when Teresa knelt beside her to say goodbye, my grandmother came back from wherever she was, jerked her head around to my sister, and exclaimed, "Teresa! My angel. I knew you would come!"

I wasn't in the room, but two of my aunts who were still recall the profundity of that moment, their mother's strange and sudden clarity, and the sense of awe with which she regarded my sister. It was as if my grandmother had seen a glimpse of the next world and knew Teresa was an extraordinary soul who would do extraordinary things.

Over the years, June 8 became a date of great significance for Teresa. Whenever an upcoming key event would occur on that date, Teresa would always say, "June 8 is Grammy's day. All will be well." It would be the date she passed her medical boards, met influential people, achieved important milestones, or found clarity and serenity during times of chaos and confusion.

And, as if to authenticate Teresa's miraculous manifestation, June 8 was also the date I moved her children into that impossible dream house with me.

Chapter 58

Help

I don't want to do this.

With every box I packed and every toss into the dumpster, that was the repeating thought in my mind. Reality hit me hard. How could I possibly give up my freedom? I didn't want to be responsible for raising two kids. I didn't want to have to cook dinner every night for two gluten-free, dairy-free, organic, non-GMO-eating vegetarians. I didn't want to search for private schools, check backpacks, and review homework. I didn't want to go to parent-teacher conferences or sell pies and cookie dough for school fundraisers. I didn't want to struggle through college applications. I didn't want any of it.

Don't get me wrong, I was beyond grateful the kids were willing to leave Florida and that I could relieve my mother and bring our family together. I just hadn't had the time to process the fallout. I felt ill-prepared for the overwhelming task that lay ahead. On top of it, the thought of leaving my home, where I had lived most of my life, left me with a feeling of dread.

My freedom would soon be over.

The new house was big and beautiful by any standard, but it was cold. The high ceilings and the large open spaces of the contemporary style overwhelmed me. I didn't know how I was going to furnish it. Most of my furniture was either antique or worn out and needed to be tossed. My style was shabby chic, which worked beautifully in my former abode, but almost nothing but my bedroom set was going to work in this house.

For the first three months, we lived in roughly six thousand square feet with virtually no furniture except for a kitchen table with six chairs, a large round ottoman, eight dining room chairs, and a ping-pong table. It took two months for the kids' new bedroom furniture to arrive.

Each room was stacked with unpacked boxes that I didn't know what to do with and had no desire to deal with. I couldn't even do the bare minimum to make the place comfortable or presentable. The only place I felt comfortable was in my bed, and I dreaded getting out of it each morning.

To top it off, we had to get our old house prepared so we could rent out our first floor or sell it—another stressful decision I struggled with daily. My husband worked for nearly four months to paint every room, rip out carpet, refinish floors, replace trim, fix windows, fill dumpsters, and get things up to code.

Finally, I had to go in and clean every corner from top to bottom. With every inch that I cleaned and every cabinet I papered, I cried. No, I wailed. I didn't want to leave the peace and comfort I depended on in my beloved home. I felt like I was leaving behind my best friend. I had lived there most of my life on and off. Memories of my sister were in every corner. I had spent the last eighteen years creating the most beautiful energy in it with my husband and my son. For me, living in that house was like being cradled in a loving hug, a warm embrace that awaited me every time I pulled into the driveway each night after work.

Now, when I walked through the door at 5:30, I stepped into a large, empty, stark, blank canvas that gave me nothing and demanded every bit of my creativity and imagination. I felt like I had been unplugged from my power source and everything else that once filled me with a sense of joy and peace. I was overwhelmed and depleted. What little energy I had, I needed to give to Jo and Carm. They needed guidance, love, healthy food, furniture, entertainment, friends, and so much more than I'd ever dared to imagine.

I needed to get my shit together.

Chapter 59

Home

I was vibrating in fear mode at every turn, and subsequently continued to create more situations that caused me stress. Talk about the law of attraction working overtime! I knew I wouldn't be able to bring forth what I wanted and needed until I removed whatever it was that was holding me back at the subconscious level. And one of the things that I love about the PSYCH-K process is that I didn't need to know *what* was holding me back. I only needed to identify what I *wanted* instead of what I was *experiencing*. But I was vibrating so low, I couldn't seem to do that on my own.

I'd never been good at reaching out for help, but I was so desperate that I swallowed my pride and sent an SOS email to about ten colleagues with whom I'd sometimes exchange sessions. I put it right out there that I wouldn't be able to return the favor. This was a rescue mission. Three facilitators got back to me immediately, and I booked time with each of them. I can still remember some of the goal statements I created:

I welcome changes in my life.
I bring the same loving energy from my old home into my new home.
I know what to do, and I do it.
I am focused.
I am calm and relaxed.

Almost immediately I was filled with a sense of peace. The pit in my stomach that greeted me each morning was gone. I felt stable! And that alone was a huge change and filled me with immense gratitude. I was able to create a to-do list and set priorities. The resistance I had been feeling about all of my new responsibilities was gone. Instead of going 'round in circles, I moved forward with more ease than I thought I was capable of.

There were so many decisions to be made for the kids, the new house, and my old house, and to my delight, I was not only able to make those decisions with ease, but I was now strong enough to do my own PSYCH-K balances any time I felt resistance about anything!

Everything started to shift for me in the direction I needed! I found the perfect private school for Jo and got her started on her application essays. I enrolled Carm in summer camp down the street so he could make friends before going to the local junior high. I made the decision to rent my house, created a lease, and published ads, and the perfect tenant moved in on October 1.

Almost immediately, the empty boxes and scattered sheets of bubble wrap that overwhelmed me no longer threatened my sanity. I was surprised at how easily I dove into action, just like the old Annie who knew how to get things done.

I still didn't have any furniture, but I felt a surge of creativity inside me and started working with what I had. Maybe I'll bookend these two orphaned captain chairs on the sides of the fireplace. I don't know what to do with that big tufted ottoman, but for now I'll just put it in front of the fireplace and create a cozy space. I cut hydrangeas from the lush landscaping that surrounded the property, put them in pretty vases, and placed them about. I lit candles and burned incense.

The house was far from furnished, but the vibe was inviting and loving and inspired me to think about what furniture and decor might work.

The kitchen was open and faced a small, odd-shaped den with a fireplace. I had no idea how to work with either space. One day—with no intention of looking for furniture—I found an adorable love seat, bought it immediately, and placed it in the den.

And the most bizarre thing happened.

As soon as I committed to that one piece of furniture, it became like a magnet attracting everything I needed. Momentum took over. Perfect pieces of furniture and decorative accents seemed to show up every-where—either inexpensively or from someone giving it to me. A pair of lamps and two sets of club chairs—two curved tangerine ones for the den and two boxy midnight-blue ones for the adjacent sunroom—on an online marketplace. A magnificent mahogany dining room table from my cousin Cindy with two leaves to seat the whole family, custom-framed artwork from my Uncle Jim, coffee tables, end tables —you name it. Antiques that I thought would never work found their proper spaces. I seemed to know just what I needed and exactly where to put it. Pictures were hung. Photos were placed. Treasured pieces were displayed.

In less than two months after working with my subconscious, I manifested an absolutely beautiful home that looked as though I had lived in it for five years. I was astounded. My family was astounded. Everyone who had watched me transform from a zombie to a woman on a mission was astounded.

I remember walking out of my bedroom one Saturday morning in late September. The sun was bursting through my home's many windows. The countless trees in the seventy acres of nature preserve that abut-ted our backyard were starting to change colors. I passed through each room, taking in its beauty and feeling the loving energy. I did it, I thought. I had the power within me all along. All I had to do was re-write the cycling emotions of fear and anxiety stored in my subconscious into what I wanted instead. The moment I did, I became vibrationally aligned with my conscious desires. I created a frequency within me that transmitted out to the Universe, where everything I wished for already existed.

And, bam! Just like Dorothy, I was home.

Chapter 60

By Your Side

It was after dinner, and the kids had just finished doing the dishes. I relished the quiet that followed. Dinnertime could be stressful. It generally started off well, but there was always an undercurrent of tension that made it difficult to let even the slightest provocations slide by unnoticed. By the time we got to the part where we were trying to remember whose turn it was to wash and whose turn it was to dry, arguments would ensue, and I had to sort them out. It was exhausting. Yet, compared to everything else I was dealing with, dinnertime was a walk in the park. Between the lack of trust, the trauma, and the grief, coming together as a family—to be brutally honest—was honestly brutal for all of us.

The kids were upstairs now, and Petr and I had retreated to our bedroom. I put on some music and lay on the bed while Petr soaked in our jacuzzi bathtub, each of us decompressing in our own way. When "By Your Side" by Sade began playing, I was quickly transported to 2000, the year Petr and I had serendipitously met in Phoenix, Arizona. (That's an incredible story all its own.)

During that time, I had been playing Sade's *Lovers Rock* album repeatedly and always associated Petr with it. As I lay there on the bed with Petr only a few feet away in the tub, I made the conscious decision to escape my current life and go on a journey in my mind to the beginning of our relationship, that magical time when our love was new. Snapshots of special moments surfaced, creating a slideshow that made my heart melt. No man had ever gotten to me like Petr.

I allowed myself to delve deeply into the memories, wanting to remember and feel it all.

It had been a long time since Petr and I were that connected. Our relationship had taken a serious hit after Teresa was murdered, and given our newly inherited responsibilities, I had serious doubts that we would ever recover. It wasn't long before I was in tears.

Then the weirdest thing happened.

Teresa appeared in the middle of my slideshow.

I was completely taken by surprise, but more than anything, I was confused. Why was she hijacking my slideshow in my special Petr song that had nothing whatsoever to do with her? She looked at me, smiled, and cleared away my slideshow with her hands. I heard her say, "This song has the perfect words that you need to hear from me right now."

And indeed, it did.

The song asks, "Do you think I'd leave your side?" And it goes on to reassure me that she'd never leave me down on my knees, and whenever I'm feeling low, she'll be there by my side. She was right. Those were just the words I needed to hear. And they were the words that kept me going on the most difficult days when I felt defeated and couldn't manage my new parental responsibilities.

"Did you really just do that, or did I make that up myself?" I asked her telepathically. I didn't need to ask because her presence was felt deeply. I started to weep uncontrollably. I knew she was with me.

But I asked her anyway, "Can you give me a sign so I know I'm not imagining all of this in my head?"

As usual, Teresa wasted no time.

What the . . .

It was Petr who snapped me out of this mental banter with my sister, " Babe, come look at this!" I felt like I already knew what he was going to say. I opened my eyes and turned my head toward the bathroom. Directly above the Jacuzzi tub was a four-candle light fixture that was turning on and off repeatedly.

I didn't want to break the connection I had with Teresa, so I asked him to be still for a moment and told him that I'd explain what was going on in a second.

I turned my attention back to Teresa.

Her timing was incredible, naturally. I knew she would never leave my side. She had been at the dinner table with us earlier, watching over her children, and would continue to guide me as I raised them in her place. Teresa would always support me, guide me, and inspire me to make the best possible choices in a particular moment, or simply reassure me that I was going in the right direction. I needed her strength and guidance to help me do right by her kids.

Since she was practically old enough to talk, Teresa had told me what to do. She always took care of me, and she still was. I knew she delivered the house we were all living in and was the creative force behind so many Divine synchronicities that provided me with exactly what this new family needed in perfect timing.

"Babe, it's not stopping," my husband called from the bathroom. I opened my eyes again and lay there silently with my head turned to the blinking light. "Look at you, Dill," I said to her in my mind, easing back into our familiar earthly relationship. The bathroom lights had been slowly blinking on and off for a while, and the song would be ending soon.

I had an idea.

"Tre," I said silently. "You know what would be really cool? A grand finale light show?"

I got off the bed, walked into the bathroom, and stared up at the light. Petr was wondering what I was doing. "Shh, hang on a second," I said, staring up at the light. The song was just about to end, and I knew with everything in me that she would indeed figure out a grand finale.

And, of course, she did.

As soon as the song ended, the slow, metered blinking kicked into a spastic light show of rapid flashing light. It reminded me of a fireworks display finale. It went on for about seven seconds, and then it stopped abruptly. It felt like she was right there in the bathroom with us.

Through my tears, I told Petr what had transpired in my mind with Teresa. He looked up at the light that was no longer blinking and stared at it with a big grin on his face. I could tell he was thinking of something to say to her. "Teresa? You will be playing with my lights?" And then he burst into his signature full-bellied Czech laugh, a laugh that always made Teresa laugh just as hard. "Gotta love that man's laugh," she'd always say. But since she hadn't yet figured out how to talk to us from the dead yet, she did something quite clever. She matched every "hah, hah, hah, hah, hah," that escaped from Petr's mouth with a blink of that light in perfect time. I joined in.

The three of us were laughing together, as naturally and exuberantly as we always had.

Chapter 61

Free at Last

It was January 2020 when Mark's death sentence was officially confirmed by the court. I am not a proponent of the death penalty, but it was important to me that Sievers would never get out of jail. Not because of justice. Not because he deserved to rot in hell. But because I needed to be sure that in the unlikely event he won an appeal, the worst-case scenario would result in a reduced sentence of life in prison without parole. Bottom line, I didn't want even the slightest potential to exist that he could see the light of day in the kids' lifetimes. When the death sentence came through, I felt great relief.

Now, with all three monsters behind bars, we could exhale. Justice had indeed been served, and knowing we didn't have to look over our shoulder or worry that Mark would try to take the kids created a deep sense of peace my family hadn't felt in almost five years. I hadn't realized how oppressed I had felt until the moment I knew he would never leave prison. I felt as if I had been carrying fifty pounds of weight on my back, and now I could finally put it down. I felt so free, and had no idea this was just the beginning.

Only a few months earlier, in October, when I was attending the first trial, my company had offered a separation package to a large population of the workforce. Without thinking twice, I took it. It was time for me to take my business to the next level and allow it to sustain my life, but more importantly, carry out my and Teresa's mission.

My last day in cubicle land was February 19, 2020, and in perfect Divine timing, I was scheduled to speak at a health-and-wellness trade show on February 29. The synchronicities were perfect. I loved how quickly I would be jumping right into my work. And with Dr. Bernie Siegel—author, retired surgeon, and pioneer of holistic medicine—as keynote speaker, I was over the moon with excitement to share the same space with this man. I love working one-on-one with clients, but speaking to large crowds excites the performer in me.

As the first speaker, I knew it was important to set the stage for the alternative practitioners, tools, and therapies introduced at the event. Like all of you who are reading this book, I wanted the audience to remain open and curious about what was possible before I launched into my presentation about the powerful subconscious and PSYCH-K. But I also wanted to excite them. So I went back to my acting days and wrote a powerful, inspirational opening monologue.

I felt aligned to the mission. I had taken the plunge to leave the security of a full-time job, leaping out of a plane without a parachute, trusting the Universe to catch me. I couldn't wait to speak at more events. I couldn't wait to reach the masses. I couldn't wait to serve humanity and be part of the change that was coming. I was on fire. I was so ready.

Two weeks later the world shut down.

Chapter 62

Chaos

When we are in a place of fear, we can only attract more situations of the same frequency. The rabbit-eared antennas, remember? That's where the people of planet earth plunged in March of 2020. Unfortunately, years later, we're even worse off.

I have to admit, my initial reflex was primal too. But amid the chaos and fear, confusion and isolation, and grief and loss, it seemed—at first—something positive was emerging from this collective experience of isolation: a universal compassion that bound us all together. But before it could take root, fear spiked up again, taking on new expressions.

Was it a pandemic or "plandemic?" Were you for the black or the blue? Left or Right? His and her or they and them? Vaccine or no vaccine? Hell, we even turned the clocks back on pro-choice. And things just kept getting worse. People started taking sides. There was no tolerance for differing opinions. Lines were drawn in the sand. Families were divided. Friends became enemies. The anger, and even hatred, was palpable. What would it take to end all this madness? It felt like the beginning of the end.

I thought about my and Teresa's apocalyptic dreams. Maybe we weren't supposed to sit around and wait for Jesus to come and clean up this mess. Maybe we were supposed to clean it up. But how? The answer came to me easily. Intuitively.

Love.

It was Teresa who introduced me to the work of internationally renowned Japanese scientist Dr. Masaru Emoto. In his book *The Hidden Messages in Water*, Dr. Emoto takes two ice crystals from severely polluted water. He blesses one of the crystals, but not the other. The results are astounding. When viewed through a microscope, the crystal that was not blessed looks like a diseased cell. But the one he blessed looks like a brilliant diamond. He repeated this process along with variations of the same idea. Some crystals would be labeled with the word *love* and another *hate*, or *beautiful* and *ugly*. The results were the same. The crystals labeled with love-based intentions shone like brilliant diamonds, while the crystals labeled with fear-based words looked like unhealthy cells.

Emoto's experiments with water were my initiation into the world of quantum physics. I saw a connection between science and mysticism.

We were designed to transmit the vibration of love throughout the Universe; the very absence of it created the situation we were in. And in the madness of 2020, I knew love was the only force powerful enough to transform humanity and change the trajectory of where we were heading. I knew a collective vibration of love could deliver us from the hellish experience we were creating on this planet.

I just knew it.

And with each day that passed, it became increasingly clear to me that if we didn't start to get our act together, we were never going to get to the other side of this shit show.

At the deepest part of my being, I felt compelled to talk to people about the healing power of love. Plant a mustard seed. But man oh man, I was scared to speak up. I know, right? Me. The performer, the speaker, the woman who's not afraid to raise her hand and say, "Excuse me, but this is really f'd up. Can we fix this, please? Thank you."

And that's exactly why I knew I had to speak up.

But tensions were high. I didn't want to offend or alienate people. Obviously, if I dared to say something or post something publicly, half the people were going to disagree with me, and probably unfriend me. I knew that. There was so much hostility on social media. Besides, what was I supposed to say? How was I supposed to explain to people that a collective vibration of love was powerful enough to transport this planet into a frequency where none of this chaos can vibrationally exist?

Maybe I didn't have to explain it.

And maybe that's why Jesus didn't explain it in 30 AD, because nobody would've understood what the hell he was talking about. So Jesus skipped the quantum physics lecture.

He had a better idea, a simple act that defied time and space and would deliver us from peril. And much to the disappointment of Peter and a few other apostles, it was not to take up arms against Rome. His message to humanity would surpass his death and survive throughout the ages:

> *Love one another as I have loved you.*
> *—John 13:34*

(As I finished writing that Bible verse, I realized that today is Good Friday. Coincidence? Nah. I feel like Jesus just gave me a high-five.)

Chapter 63

A Message of Love

I love my car. It's a 2017 Honda Accord—loaded—white with tan leather interior. It's a real beauty. What I love the most about it, though, is the car stereo. Even as a teenager, whenever my master-mechanic-of-a-dad would get me a used car, or shit-box, the first thing I would do was figure out how I was going to afford to install an 8-track player, a pair of Jenson coaxial speakers, and subwoofers. I could have cared less how many miles the car had or what kind of gas mileage it got. *I want to blast my tunes, Dad.*

It was sometime in September of 2020. I had set out to run some errands, dreading the masked faces and frightful eyes I would meet at every stop. I hated going out these days. I wasn't afraid of getting sick; I was sick of all the fear that was literally making people sick. Most of all, I was deeply saddened to witness humanity's loss of connection. It continued to feel like the end of the world, or at the very least, that the life we all once knew was over.

The crusader spirit within me was urging me to make a stand, as if it was my responsibility. I felt compelled to spread love in some way, however small—even a tiny pebble of an act could create waves. Daily, I pondered what I could possibly do. I even thought about designing T-shirts with a message of love—something that would get people's attention, create a spark, or change their perception of what's possible. Maybe I could coin a clever phrase or graphic to change people's hearts. Remember the "Love is . . ." statues from the '70s? Something like that. I envisioned everything from creating an online presence to setting a table outside of a grocery store where I could give away this phantom creation. I even thought about taking out an ad or a billboard space. Somewhere there's a piece of scrap paper with my musings of various taglines that I hoped would go viral.

I had only just gotten out of my driveway and about halfway down the cul-de-sac when my car stereo went berserk. Now, I don't know about your car, but whenever I start my car, my phone—assuming I have it in the car, of course—will automatically go to Bluetooth and start playing either my music library or whatever book app I was last listening to. On this particular day, it was my music library that turned on, only it wouldn't stop on a song. Instead, titles of songs flashed by one after another in the display as if someone was holding their finger down on the Forward button. This went on for about ten seconds or so, until it finally stopped on the song "Message of Love" by the Pretenders.

I knew immediately this message was for me from my sister.

But always one to test the magical skills of the Universe and wanting to be sure this wasn't just a one-time fluke, I hit the next button again to see what would happen. Once again song titles appeared one after another so quickly I barely had enough time to finish reading the title before the next song appeared.

This time it stopped on "Interstate Love Song." I noted the love connection in the titles and then hit the 'next' arrow again. Song titles once again quickly appeared and disappeared on my display until they finally stopped on "Message of Love" for a second time. I repeated this processes at least a dozen times and continued to jump from "Interstate Love Song" back to "Message of Love."

I looked over at the passenger seat like I often did and imagined Teresa sitting there with one finger on the 'fast forward arrow' and a shit-eating grin on her face. It wasn't a big leap to make.

A few days later, I headed out to run some errands again, this time with Teresa's kids, Carm and Jo. As usual, my phone immediately connected with my car's Bluetooth, and again connected directly to my personal song library. Once again, song titles began to speed through my display. I startled the kids from their phones. "Guys, check this out!" I said. They looked up from their devices as I pointed to the display that was once again scanning through my song library. I eagerly awaited to see what song it would stop on.

It was "Message of Love," again.

"Now watch this," I said with a sense of anticipation as if I was about to perform a magic trick. I hit the 'next' arrow. The same strange flurry of titles appeared and disappeared on my screen and stopped on "Message of Love." "You guys, this is so crazy!" I squealed. "This same thing happened to me the other day."

Neither impressed nor interested, they grunted something about something and then went back to posting, snapping, texting, or whatever it was they were doing with their phones.

When it was obvious that my song library was only offering "A Message of Love," Carm asked if he could please connect his phone to my Bluetooth, end all this strangeness with my stereo, and expose me to his finer musical tastes. Doubtful that would actually be the case, I side glanced him in the passenger seat next to me with a sarcastic smile. He returned the sentiment and proceeded to connect his phone to my Bluetooth. I sat there getting ready to cringe in anticipation of Carm's music.

Instead, I watched my display flash with songs and stop on "Message of Love."

Assuming his phone must not have connected properly, Carm tapped away at the display screen. Again, I braced myself for Carm's music repertoire.

But "Message of Love" was coming through my speakers.

Carm was getting annoyed, Jo was telling him he was stupid and didn't know how to set up his Bluetooth, and Carm was telling Jo to shut up. I knew an argument was going to break out at any moment, so I interrupted.

"Guys, it's your mom doing this." Having also experienced weirdness and wonderfulness with their mother, they agreed it was probably her, but weren't particularly interested in this moment. "Great. Can you tell her to stop messing with my music!" Carm said with a mixture of humor and annoyance.

Teenagers.

Once again, Carm went back to my Bluetooth menu, selected his name from the display, and double-checked his phone settings.
But "Message of Love" would not stop playing.

Carm was exasperated. "I'm done messing with this thing," he snapped. He scrolled through the car's display screen, found "Carm's iPhone," and deleted it from the Bluetooth device list. We drove the rest of the way in silence.

About ten minutes later, we stopped off at our favorite organic market —that unfortunately closed a few months ago—grabbed some groceries and our favorite "Teresa-approved" healthy snacks, and then headed back to the car. I started the engine and wondered if hooking up Carm's phone and then disconnecting it from my Bluetooth would somehow interfere with Teresa's deejaying efforts.

But it didn't.

Just as before, song titles flashed through my display and stopped on "Message of Love" and began to play. And that's when I noticed something about my new car that I hadn't noticed before. The display shows the name of the device it's connected to in smaller letters. Currently, the display showed "Carm's iPhone" was connected. "Carm, Look! Your phone *is* connected to the Bluetooth, but my library is playing. How is that happening?"

Jo chimed in with some insight, but Carm told her to shut up and fished his phone from his pocket. "Fine. I'll turn off the Bluetooth from my phone. Something must be wrong with your car's Bluetooth." No, I thought to myself, this is definitely Teresa. Carm interrupted my thoughts, "What the hell? My Bluetooth is already off!" I looked at Carm and beamed, "Isn't this incredible?" He looked at me and rolled his eyes, "Whatever."

I turned up the radio and, much to the chagrin of Carm and Jo, sang along with Chrissie Hynde and her "Message of Love," all the while with "Carm's iPhone" aglow in my display.

"Well, the reason we're here . . . is to love each other. Take care of each other . . ."

Chapter 64

We All Have That One Sister

After my sister was murdered, the love my friends poured upon me was a salve like no other. They knew, or at least they tried to imagine, my anguish. Sometimes the best any of them could offer was silence. What could anyone possibly say or do for me, really?

Except maybe make me laugh. Now there's a healing vibe.

I still remember when that text came in from Zito. I was sitting on my sofa back at the old Victorian house, probably watching some movie in the hopes it would provide the numbing effect I longed for.

I opened the text and busted out in laughter. The only other person who could make me laugh that hard was my sister. And the meme Zito sent me was testimony to that.

The image was of two girls. On the right sat a young girl with long dark hair who appeared to be about ten years old. A younger girl to her right with blonde hair looked to be about five years old. These two girls could have been me and Teresa. And even though Zito didn't know either of us at that age, I know why he thought the same thing.

The younger sister, with an appearance of justifiable righteousness, boldly and proudly held her right fist in front of her with only her middle finger raised, while the older one looked at the camera in shock, amusement, and perhaps a tinge of fear that someone was going to get in big trouble.

The caption read, "We all have that one sister."

And indeed, I had that sister. Precisely.

I don't know anyone who could flip the bird quite like Teresa. She did it with an air of calm and unusual versatility. It was her hallmark expression. She almost never gave the finger in the throes of anger, but rather as an amusing gesture. Perhaps we got lost in a crowd at a concert, or I couldn't find my way back to the blanket at the beach or an outdoor festival. If Teresa spotted me first, rather than approaching me to say, "Oh, there you are," or waving her hand with a helpful, "I'm over here," she would stay back and watch me scan the crowd and wait for me to notice her. And when I finally did spot her, it became obvious she was anticipating my discovery with a subtle smirk on her face and her middle finger casually raised in my direction.

Or she might use the middle finger to celebrate a victory in some way. Like the time she was visiting in Connecticut and wanted to go on a bike ride with my brother Patrick. Pat had a ten-speed, but all he could offer Teresa was his daughter's basic, banana-seat bike. Teresa insisted she'd be fine riding on the banana seat without any gears to help her navigate the big hills that surrounded us. After all, she was in better shape than any of us. But those hills were daunting. And without gears? I never would have attempted such a feat. But this, of course, was Teresa, so off the two of them went.

"How'd it go?" I said when they returned. Teresa glided by me and casually refilled her water bottle, Pat right behind her, somewhat winded but laughing. "Ann, we were going up this hill. It was a little tough for me on the ten-speed, and I wondered how Teresa was going manage it with that piece-of-shit bike. Two minutes later, she passes right by me and doesn't say a word, just raises her arm in the air, flips me the bird, and flies by."

It was classic.

But my favorite Teresa flipping-of-the-bird story was the time I was on northbound Interstate 95 in Connecticut heading from Norwalk to Ansonia. This was a forty-minute drive that generally took two hours on a Friday during rush hour. As usual, it was bumper to bumper for miles and miles. So naturally, I tried to amuse myself with music and chain smoking. This was about 1988, so the Marlboro Lights were aplenty.

After singing along unabashedly to one side of my Anita Baker cassette and barely moving, I fixed in on the car in front of me that I'd been crawling behind for the last thirty minutes or so. It was a fairly new white Hyundai Sonata, but it was dirty and a little banged up. "Kind of looks like Teresa's car," I mused to myself. I tried to get closer, thinking I might be able to see the driver or at least an arm or something that would confirm my suspicion.

Finally, I crept closer to her back bumper to get a better look. What I didn't know was that Teresa had long ago spotted me in her rearview mirror, as I gave my free concert on I-95, and was now watching me as I discovered the faint Fairfield University stenciled on her back window. At precisely the moment I realized it was her, Teresa, never turning her head around, slowly raised her right arm between the bucket seats with her middle finger straight up in the air.

Now fast-forward to my Bluetooth going bonkers and playing "Message of Love" in my car. A couple of days after that happened, I was sitting in front of my vanity, getting ready for an online session with a client. As usual, I had my phone by my side, although I hadn't yet chosen a music app, nor had I reached out to Teresa with any questions or specific intentions. But I couldn't stop thinking about the bizarre incident with my car's Bluetooth. There was no question Teresa had synced up with my desire to create a message of love; she couldn't have been more direct by picking a song with the same title. And directness was definitely her style.

I tapped a music app, put my phone down on the granite-topped vanity, and fumbled around in the drawer for my moisturizer. The moment I heard the first few notes of the synthesizer, I felt a stirring within me. And when Lou Gramm began to sing, "I want to know what love is," a few measures later, I was overcome with emotion and chills. I knew that meant that the song was a message for me. It was the "I want you to show me," and, "I know you can show me," lyrics that really got me. I felt that urgency to show people what love was or what love could do. But how?

The next song answered the question for me, as Michael McDonald's signature, sexy voice sang out to "Takin' It to the Streets."

Later that night, I awoke from a deep sleep and downloaded the following poem in just a few minutes:

A Warrior for Love

Take a moment.
Be still.
The time has come.
Listen.
Let's create this.
A place of love and peace.
Where we feel safe.
Yet empowered.
Where we're happy.
Joyful.
Embracing our divinity.
How?
Choose Love.

Take a moment.
Find the feeling that gets you "there."
The bittersweet beauty of feeling the light
within you and
never wanting it to extinguish.
Love like there's a million tomorrows
of the best day you've ever had.
Love like there's no tomorrow.

Take a moment.
Throw away your pride.
Detach from taking sides.
Go inward.
Find it.
Know it.
Feel it.
Expand it.
Exalt it.
Vibrate it.
Choose Love.

Go deep.
Deeper.
Find the compassion.
Let it explode.
Like golden rays from your heart.
Reaching out to everyone you see or think about.
Yes.
Everyone.
Especially the ones you don't like.
Choose Love.

Take a moment.
Share it.

Copy it.
Talk about it.
Laugh about it.
A hard belly laugh that brings tears to your eyes.
Write about.
Sing about it.
Dance about it.
Beat a drum.
Become a Warrior for Love.

Stay in the rhythm.
Of love.
But do it.
Now.
And the moment you catch yourself not doing it.
Start doing it.
Again.
Keep doing it.
Choose Love.

Love thy neighbor. — JC (Jesus Christ)
All you need is love. — JL (John Lennon)
Love heals. — TS (Teresa Sievers)

I love you.
Unconditionally. — A.L. (Annie Lisa)

I felt so much lighter after I wrote it, but I wasn't done. Now, I was supposed to take it to the streets, which I knew meant posting it on social media. And I was still afraid to do that. I didn't think it was a great poem, but I also felt like maybe that was another message for me. Maybe posting a mediocre poem was required because it forced me to take the risk of facing mockery and ridicule. And it forced me to surrender and trust my intuition at the cost of my ego.

I stared at my Facebook home page's, "What's on your mind, Annie?" and carefully pasted my poem to the feed. I held my breath and tapped that blue Post button. There it was. But only for a second. My phone screen went black. When it lit up again, a photo popped up from my photo album.

The blonde-haired girl was grinning at me and giving me the finger.

Chapter 65

Revelations

I have no idea what the incredible odds were of hearing "Aquarius"—a song released in 1969—that day in September 2014 when I abandoned my bank errand for a jaunt at a thrift store instead. But never have I doubted the purpose of the song: an affirmative answer to the question I'd asked only moments before in my car, "Is this song a message for me?"

Something about the occurrence of "Message of Love" reminded me of that day.

I knew Teresa was playing deejay to acknowledge the obligation I felt to reunite people with love. It was her way of saying, "Yes. You're on the right track, girl. Love is the way out." And to make that message really stand out, she played the song while Carm's phone was connected.

Then it hit me.

The soft, authoritative voice that interrupted my thoughts moments after I asked God why the song "Aquarius" was making me cry uncontrollably. The voice that summoned me into the parking lot of a store instead of the bank. The voice that answered me back when I objected that I didn't have time to try on clothes, and told me to stand in the back and try on shoes instead.

The voice that told me to go to My Sister's Place.

Wait! *My Sister's* Place?

MY sister? Oh my God! My sister Teresa!

In my mind, I saw three-year-old Teresa in her ponytails, swinging her dangling feet as she sat on the potty. Hadn't she tried to explain things to me that she couldn't possibly have known? Memories from before her birth? Future events?

And what about our last weekend together? Those prophetic remarks. The heartburn that made her feel like she was going to die. Telling her children only hours before her murder that someday she would be dead and that she needed to know that she'd taught them everything they needed to know.

Teresa didn't consciously know what was unfolding, but she reacted to it nonetheless with feistiness and impatience. It was an inner knowing that permeated just beneath the surface, creating a constant, conflicting sense of Divine duty and impending doom. It's why she worked so tirelessly and fiercely to shake up the medical world with a healing paradigm that freed people from their dependency on pharmaceutical drugs and empowered them to heal themselves. It's why she relentlessly nagged me to write my book, and in death, wrote it with me.

Could it have been my sister's infinite spirit that sent me to My Sister's Place? Had our eternal souls long ago planned that experience? What if I hadn't tuned into the chills and tears evoked by repeatedly playing that song? What if I hadn't asked the Universe to help me understand the power that song seemed to have over me? I could have ignored the voice that told me to go to My Sister's Place. I might have laughed when I heard "Aquarius" playing over my head, and written all of it off as a meaningless coincidence.

All those choices were mine to make.

I could have dismissed all of it.

But I didn't.

I'm not telling you this because I want you to think I'm special. That's my mother's job.

I'm telling you this because you're special.

We're all special.

We all chose to be here now during this incredible time on the planet. And many people reading this already understand that. If you don't, then I hope by now, as you reach the end of this book, you will.

Chapter 66

The Age of Aquarius

Astrology is actually one of the oldest sciences, and throughout history, it has proven to have incredible relevance in predicting cycles and patterns. Though most people limit astrology to the personality traits of the sign they were born under or their daily horoscopes, for others, their cuckoo la-la meter tends to go off.

Personally, I don't bother looking at my horoscope, because our astrological sign alone plays only one very small part in determining what is on the horizon for us, not to mention our numerology.

Astrology is very complicated stuff. Any good astrologer will tell you that it takes many, many years of study to understand how the energetic frequencies of the planets, planetary aspects, nodes, houses, degrees, starts, and so much more influence our human potential.

The planetary phenomena that astrology predicts cannot be explained by classical science or even physics. However, quantum physics, which looks at the interconnectedness of particles at their subatomic level, certainly sheds some light. At its very core, research in quantum physics suggests that we are all connected through quantum entanglement. That means that you cannot fully evaluate or understand the cosmos without considering the physical world or humanity. Likewise, you cannot fully evaluate or understand humanity without considering the cosmos. Everything affects everything.

The Age of Aquarius is created when the energetic fields of Saturn and Jupiter, along with the constellation known as Aquarius, are positioned in such a way that they create an energetic field that supports the expansion of mindfulness, consciousness, and empowerment. All of this provides an opportunity for humanity to awaken to its true nature.

Love.

According to many astrologers, the Age of Aquarius officially began in December 2020, not coincidentally a defining moment in our history and human experience due to Covid and its aftermath. It is a time of great upheaval in virtually every aspect of our lives, a time that demands an expansion of consciousness for our survival.

When we will actually start to feel the effects from this harmonious Age is debatable. There are a range of predictions that suggest it could be another ten or fifteen years. And I believe the lack of consensus is due to the unpredictability of our participation in the birthing of this age. As I assess the state of the world today, it appears that this could be a long and painful labor.

But it doesn't have to be.

Chapter 67

The Mission

Life is speeding by faster than ever. We blink, and another year is over. This is not your imagination. As we move into the Age of Aquarius, a higher vibrational frequency also referred to as the *fifth dimension*, the illusion of time is collapsing. We can see this unfolding in our daily lives.

Think about it.

Only a few decades ago, if you wanted to invite fifty people to your house for a party, you had to get in your car and go to the store to purchase invitations and then handwrite fifty invitations. You more than likely had to call a few people or haul out a phone book for addresses, put them in the mail, and wait for them to reach their destination. And in order to get the RSVP, you had to physically be home to answer your phone, and keep the line free so you could receive those incoming calls.

Today, you grab your cell phone, and you're done in seconds.

You want a pair of shoes? Tap a few buttons and, viola! A blue van pulls into your driveway and delivers them to you the next day.
Through technology, we are getting a preview of how quickly the law of attraction will manifest our subconscious thoughts into this new dimensional frequency. Your thoughts will become reality more quickly than ever. You've probably noticed it happening. Those

moments of thinking about someone or needing something? And then both appear in no time?

Exactly.

That's why how you show up vibrationally in your life matters now more than ever. Because before you can finish thinking it or feeling it, it's happening. This is why internal housekeeping is critical.

Specifically, we need to remove the fear-based beliefs our subconscious has been using to create instructions and directions for our behavior without our conscious knowledge. It's time to clean up our operating system and delete programs that keep us stuck in the same patterns. These programs have created our lives and the world we live in and are operating in the background 95 percent of the day without our conscious consent. If you get nothing from this book at all, this one critical truth is the key takeaway.

How you clean up your subconscious is up to you. Teresa led me to PSYCH-K. It is simple, safe, and powerful. It has been taught to hundreds of thousands in over sixty countries and translated into over twenty languages. It's what my sister told me to use, and it's what Bruce Lipton uses. Take a look. If it doesn't speak to you, find another modality that does.

But please, do it.

Those who choose to remain greedy, angry, wounded, scared, and jealous—the top five fear factors—will struggle desperately to embrace the changes that are coming our way. And we wrote this book especially for you.

When we align our subconscious with our conscious wishes and desires, not only do we live the lives we want and become happier, but in doing so, we heal our wounds. We're not the victim anymore. We're not hurt people who hurt people. We're happy. In fact, we are joyful. Our capacity to love ourselves and others unconditionally takes hold and creates a vibrational ripple effect on humanity that we can't begin to imagine.

This is the heart of my and Teresa's mission.

When we become the peace we seek, we change the trajectory of this planet and move gracefully into this new age that is upon us.

We start with ourselves from the inside out, and in doing so, we remember that we are all connected.

That's right. No one else is going to change it for us. No more pointing the fingers of blame. On a political party. On a president. On a country. No more taking sides. It's not about who is right. It's not about who wins. This is not the Super Bowl! What we are facing now is not a competition.

It is a transition that requires cooperation over competition.

Love over fear.

Love *is* the answer.

Now imagine every cell in your body and every particle of light within you is transformed by the power of love just like Emoto's droplets of water.

That's how we change the world.

Long ago, we all chose to be citizens on earth at this pivotal moment, each of us agreeing to play a role with a collective mission: to remember the Divinity within us so that we can release this planet from the illusion of separation from one another, from nature, from God, and from every particle throughout the vast Universe. Right now, the cosmos are aligned to vibrate an energetic potential to help us remember that we are all connected.

The next time you judge someone who looks, acts, or thinks differently than you do, remember that at our core, we are more alike than we are different. We all want the same things. Compassion. Love. Peace.

This is the Age of Aquarius.

Throughout my quest, I've been blessed with sublime experiences, mystical mile markers along my spiritual journey. Each has been dynamic within itself, but together they created a prism that changed my perception of reality and created a curiosity within me to continually ask, "Why am I here? What am I supposed to do?"

I'm sure you are asking the same questions. Every moment of your life, Divine guidance is available to you. It's your birthright. And as you remove your subconscious wounds, you will step into it with ease.

You can tap into it in the same way that Teresa and I did, and I continue to do. Set your intentions. Ask for confirmation, and then expect it. When coincidences appear in your life, don't ignore them; acknowledge the guidance. Each acknowledged experience will lead you to another doorway where you will have the opportunity to understand more fully the amazing, multi-dimensional being you are.

We need to walk through those doors now.

My greatest hope is that my and Teresa's experiences will spark your personal awakening and transform you into the loving Beings we were always meant to be, and now—more than ever— need to be.

This is my message of love to you.

Afterword

At some point Teresa must have realized her nagging tactics were futile and that she needed to explore other means to get me moving on our book.

It was Labor Day 2022. I was, yet again, productively procrastinating, a talent I have perfected over the years. Instead of doing what I know in my heart I am supposed to be doing, in this case get cracking on my book, I find another project of relative importance and immerse myself in it, creating utility and a false sense of accomplishment.

I was in the middle of such productive procrastination—a massive organizational project that involved yanking paperwork from every desk drawer and file cabinet I owned, until I found myself sitting in my sunroom surrounded by stacks of folders and papers. It was the type of project I had to complete before the end of the day, lest I leave mountains of private papers in the middle of my house. I was committed. I was focused. I was determined to let no one or nothing disturb me.

I still remember staring at my phone screen and seeing that my new friend, singer/songwriter Abigail Rockwell, was calling me. I clearly remember saying out loud, "Sorry my beauty, I can't talk to you now." I knew we were long overdue for an in-depth conversation, but this was not the day it was going to happen. Somehow in the middle of apologizing to her for a second time, I found myself answering the phone anyway, and silently cursing to myself for sabotaging my productive procrastination.

My connection with Abigail was immediate. She'd started out as a client a couple of years earlier and we recently became friends. Even though she's years younger than me, I look up to Abigail like an older sister.

As usual, we didn't waste any time jumping into a deep conversation, which at some point involved me discussing the nature of reality, the law of attraction and, of course, the power of our subconscious. After I'd finally stopped talking. Abigail, in her beautiful velvety voice, said, "Annie you need write a book."

Since we were new friends, Abigail was ignorant to my procrastinatory history that was keeping me from that very goal. But as an artist, she saw an opportunity to nurture my passionate propositions. Before I could acknowledge her intuition, she launched into a compelling and powerful pep talk, insisting that I needed to write a book about my work, my mission and my ongoing relationship with my sister. She spoke with such authority, it was as if Teresa herself was on the other end of the phone.

I felt like I was being Tottenized.

In the middle of Abigail's unrelenting, but loving lecture, she occasionally interjected with a comment like, "I don't know why I am saying these things to you," or "I don't usually talk like this," and "I don't mean to sound pushy." Aha, I thought. So that's why I answered the phone. 'That Teresa' had had enough of being ignored, and decided she was going to use this lovely high-vibrating vehicle, Abigail, to make her case once and for all.

When at last there was finally a pause, I filled Abigail in on my deep desire to write the very book she outlined and my equal effort to self-sabotage its creation. "Teresa has been giving me messages about exactly what you just said. I even hear her in my head. I think you were channeling her." Abigail laughed musically, agreeing that she felt like her words were coming from someone else.

Now she switched gears. Drawing from her own artistic practices and that of her famous grandfather, Norman, Abigail launched into a very helpful lesson on creative discipline. Of course that sounds like an oxymoron, but I quickly understood what she meant. "You need to get up around 3:00AM. That's magic time, Annie. That's what my grandfather did, even on Christmas day!" I whined a bit. I was an early riser, but 3:00 a.m.? "Well, you'll need to take a nap," she said casually and continued to excitedly lay out a creative regime that included getting up before dawn, journaling, meditating, yoga and countless other brilliant ideas to get me going.

The next morning, I got up at 3:00 AM and starting writing, and didn't stop until my first draft was complete.

So often through the course of writing this book, my text notification chimed at 11:11, morning and night, with a text from Abigail, who was unaware of the time and its meaning to me and Teresa. Sometimes she simply sent a purple heart, Teresa's signature color—something else of which Abigail was unaware. Other times it was words of encouragement. And, of course, there was the time she texted me a screenshot of her phone's wallpaper with an 11:11 time stamp—for no reason— at literally the exact moment I was writing about my magical night in Newark on September 28, 2014. (And as I mentioned in the book, the date was also September 28th!)

And speaking of September 28th, here is another superb synchronicity:

I was scheduled to give one of my typical talks about the subconscious and PSYCH-K at a charming farm. I had met the owner Sarah one day after being rerouted down backroads on my way back from the dentist. Sarah and I clicked immediately and she asked me if I'd like do a talk at the farm. She pointed to a white tent on the property and described how beautiful it was in the evening. Before I knew it, we created an event with dinner under the stars. I was very excited.

My typical talk included an intro about my journey, how my sister led me to the work I do with the subconscious, and PSYCH-K. Then I would flip a slide of a book cover mock-up and mention my book, and dive into my presentation. But Sarah insisted that I change the focus and include reading from sections of the book. The thought terrified me. I freaked out and told Sarah that I'd have to get back to her on that.

I needed to check in with my subconscious. I already knew my fear had to do with 'permission.' I was very apprehensive about reading this book before it was published because I didn't know what the 'rules' were. As a kid, I had been a rule-follower of the highest order. I was afraid to try new things unless I knew I had permission because I was terrified of getting into trouble. And for that, I dodged the idea of publicly reading my manuscript whenever someone suggested it to me.

I muscle tested, "I have permission to read from my manuscript before it's published." It was weak. So, I did the PSYCH-K balance, which only took about a minute. Then I muscle tested again, "I have permission to read from my manuscript before it's published." It was strong. I felt, well, fearless.

Now, feeling aligned with Sarah's suggestion that I lead our event with my book, I called Sarah back, "Let's do it!" And I've never looked back. In fact, I went ahead and booked more events without the slightest resistance about the idea. That's the power of a PSYCH-K balance; it removes the block at the subconscious level that quickly. And then bam! You're on your way baby!

After I hung up the phone with Sarah I shrieked with excitement! Mick was with me as I danced around the kitchen. "Way to go, Mom!" Then it hit me all at once. I looked at Mick, "I just realized the date of the event! Mick, the very first time I publicly read my book is the very same day Teresa and I learned about the mission in Newark! September 28th!"

I no sooner finished proclaiming that insight when the light over the kitchen island blinked off and then on. Teresa always finds a way to let me know she's working this gig from the other side. Let me back up a couple of months from this event to June 28th. This one was pretty amazing.

When the anniversary of Teresa's death comes up, or even on her birthday—two days with intense vibrational connection to her—I ask her for a sign, and I always get something from her. I wrote about the experience in this book when I recounted the one-year anniversary of her murder and how Teresa's Mass card ended up on the floor.

This past June 28th, only a few months before my first public reading, I silently said to Teresa, "Today is a tough one honey. I'm trying not to relive the day. Can you please send me a sign?" And then I went along with whatever I was doing in the kitchen. Ten minutes later I got a call from my friend Karen—a different Karen, not my wife from another life. This Karen used to work with Teresa on the nutritional side of her practice. "Dill," she said when I answered the phone. I loved when she called me that. Karen was privy to Teresa's pet name for me as I often saw her when I visited my sister.

"Did you get my text?" she asked. For some reason I hadn't heard my text alert. "No." I said. I opened her text and could not believe what I was seeing. It was a photo of a white car with the Mercedes logo prominent. The plates were Florida plates. Teresa drove a white

Mercedes with Florida plates, too. But the license plate on THIS car was "Dill 1." The message had such speed and precision.

Go ahead. I dare you to call that a coincidence.

The mental message I got from my sister when I saw that photo was, "Can I be any clearer, Dill? Just ask and I'm here." I thought about what she'd said to me in Spirit when I felt her standing behind me and holding my hands. "Ann, don't you know I'm loving you all the time?"

***

It was no surprise that Teresa's energy hovered around my dear friend Joe Zito during his first read of the manuscript. She tipped her hat to Zito, more than once.

Zito began reading my first draft on his way to Italy and concluded in Palermo Sicily where he sent me a long email at 1:37 a.m. local time. He shared his enthusiasm for my book and my mission and wanted to let me know that Teresa was with him during his travels.

At a visit to the grave of his grandfather in Sicily, a long-desired visit for Zito, he noticed the date of his grandfather's death was the same date he stood and gazed upon it for the first time. "Teresa would have appreciated this synchronicity," he said to me in his early morning email from Palermo. Then two days later, out of the blue, Zito's cousin who almost never texts him, sent him a screenshot of an 11:11 timestamp for no reason whatsoever.

Another strange thing happened when Zito went to see the plaque of Salve D'Esposito Sorrento in Rome marking his composition of *Anema e Core*. Zito's son, Michael, who was traveling with him, wanted to take a picture of his Dad standing in front of that plaque, which Zito sent later to me. Right next to Zito and the plaque was a large poster of Mother Teresa that he hadn't noticed until his son sent the picture to his phone. Not only did Mother Teresa spell her name the same as my sister without the 'H', but my own mother always referred to my sister as "little Mother Teresa." When Zito sent me the picture, I was drawn to the song title on the plaque. *Anema e Core,* which translates to "with all my heart and soul." It was the word, "Anema." It looks like Anniemae, Zito's nickname for me. It was like all three of us were in the picture.

A few days later with Zito still in Italy, and both he and Teresa in my head, my thoughts were confirmed when my phone started to act up with my car's Bluetooth, yet again.

I don't know where I was driving because I didn't record that in my journal. I pulled out of my driveway and selected a station from my Pandora on my phone and waited for one of my stations to play. A Mary J. Blige song came on.

This was strange because I didn't have a play list on Pandora with MJ on it. I looked up at my display and saw my iTunes library was playing instead, even though I knew I selected Pandora because it's on the first screen of my phone apps. The MJ song was from Teresa's memorial service playlist. *Hmm.* I figured that must have meant something, so I pressed the arrow on my steering wheel to advance to the next song. It was Zito and me from my Bus Stop Annie play list. I listened to a few bars of me belting out a Melissa Etheridge tune and advanced to the next song. The station went back to Teresa's memorial service, "All You Need is Love." I advanced again and another song from my and Zito's playlist. I advanced again, another from Teresa's memorial. Again, and it was me and Zito.

Finally I stopped hitting advance and let the songs play out, and the same pattern continued. I had to laugh. It was like Teresa created a new playlist that included the three of us. That she was with him in

Italy and hovering over him as he read the manuscript. Then I remembered the date. How could I not have made the connection sooner.

It was June 28th. Of course.

I couldn't wait to talk to Zito when he returned from Italy. "Annie," he began. "Before I even talk about the book, I have to share something. During the entire trip, it seemed like no matter what we were planning to do on a particular day, there was some sort of issue. Whether we couldn't get the right train, or a site we wanted to visit was closed, or we ended up in the wrong place, or whatever. The trip was wrought with these types of situations. And for every one of them, the issue was not only magically resolved, but dramatically improved." Zito said he was pretty sure it was Teresa helping him out, but since he was surrounded with so much familia heritage and nostalgia, he couldn't be sure. When he returned home though, he found out the name of his benefactor.

On the flight back to the United States neither his nor his son's boarding pass would scan. They were pulled out of line and sent to the desk at the gate where an agent told him they'd been upgraded to first class, a nice surprise for an eight-hour flight. The agent hadn't an explanation for the upgrade. "Annie, I've never flown first class in my life," Zito said. I smiled because I already knew where this story was going, and I couldn't wait to tell him an equally interesting one.

"This morning my son sends me a text," he continued. "He told me that he'd found our boarding passes in his carry-on, and that he thought I'd like to know that I was sitting in seat number 11.'" Zito let out joyous laughter and I joined him. "Zito," I said finally. "Are you ready for this? I've only flown first class one time, too. Years ago, I was headed back to Connecticut from Teresa's. I wasn't feeling well, so she packed up my stuff and checked me in online. When I hugged her goodbye, she said, 'Enjoy your flight, Dill. I upgraded you to first class.' "

***

By now, you've probably noticed that Teresa always gets the last word, and this book is no exception. As I prepare today to layout these pages for you, I think to myself, "I'm almost done."

Wrong.

Let me explain.

As you have read, I cherish the incredible relationship that continues between Teresa and me. I remain in awe of the blessed profundity of every one of our special moments of connection and I hold eternal gratitude for our shared mission. But I have to confess that I don't create space for her to show up in my life. What I mean is I don't sit in stillness and silence to ask, "What more can I do?"

I know I should, but I don't.

Of course, I ask for signs on her birthday or on the anniversary of her death, and I ask for signs when I'm looking for guidance. She immediately responds. She consistently flicks lights on and plays songs to confirm something that I need to know or to underscore my feelings or intentions. And with each experience I feel an energetic tug from her, a prevailing intuition that she wants to play a bigger role in my life, or that perhaps "I" need to play a bigger role in my life.

Yet I don't act upon these feelings.

One time in particular I was belaboring over social media, my least favorite marketing activity at which I am most inconsistent. I tend to overthink my post and end up doing nothing. I heard Teresa in my mind, "If you'd sit still for five minutes, I can help you." I laughed. She was right. I have my earbuds in all the time, listening to music or a book, or talking on the phone as I multi-task, a habit that prevents me from quieting my mind and listening for guidance. It felt like Teresa was telling me that she could help me with my daily posts. I heard her again, "Just sit still and I'll be there. That's all you have to do."

I was about to ask her to give me a sign, confirmation that she was really talking to me in my head, but first I stepped out of my studio to grab some water. I stopped in my tracks. The double set of hallway lights that haven't worked for a couple of years despite numerous lightbulb changes and a perplexed electrician, was ablaze with light! I turned them off and then back on to see if it was a fluke. The lights worked. I did it a bunch of times more. Again, real fast. There were no issues (and they have worked fine ever since). I asked Teresa if that was a sign of confirmation from her. I imagined she thought, "Do I really have to spell everything out for you?"

Ignoring her retort, real or imagined, I went ahead and grabbed my phone and opened the first music app that I saw. I looked at the screen anxiously awaiting her answer in the form of a song title. Her answer?

'Hallelujah!'

I read the title and laughed, imagining her voice, "Hallelujah! Finally! How many signs do you want?"

Still again, I am ashamed to say that I did not take her up on her offer.

I've always known that if Teresa and I had time to plan before her death, had she not exited from this physical plane so abruptly, she would have outlined an afterlife agenda for the two of us. I can assure you she would have sharply addressed my proclivity (at that time) to start, stop, not complete, procrastinate, and sometimes just plain half-ass it. Naturally she would have agreed to roll out our mission, but she wouldn't have stopped there. Teresa's vision was so much larger than mine. She would have foreseen a greater purpose for our ongoing connection.

She would have made me promise to regularly create space for us to connect within.

That's why the license plate on the anniversary of her death felt like a big kick in the behind from her.

You have to understand that Teresa's Spirit is many dimensions away from here; she left this physical plane more than nine years ago. She has long since transitioned, integrated and returned to her full spiritual nature. Aspects of her Spirit may even have reincarnated to other places. Teresa and I exist on very different frequencies. Yet without any candles, ritual, cleansing, sage burning, intention-setting, meditation, vibe-raising, mediumship skills or *ANYTHING,* Teresa was able to deliver a *crystal clear calling card at lightning speed:* the make and color of her car and a Florida plate inscribed with our pet name, only moments after I'd asked her for a sign.

That's what I'm talking about!

The experience was very similar to the time 'Jimmy Miller' appeared on my television screen. In the same way, I knew Teresa was seriously trying to get my attention.

And once again, I did nothing.

Then this next thing happened.

Last night I had a huge insight during an online PSYCH-K Facilitators meeting that was attended by people from all over the world. The purpose of the meeting was to inspire Facilitators to use some very special PSYCH-K protocols created by the late Rob Williams in 2018. Referred to as the "New Reality" protocols, they were created exclusively for Facilitators to deeply nurture our being and our sense of oneness with all that is. They were designed not only to elevate our consciousness, but also the consciousness of those who inhabit this planet. I knew right away that I needed to incorporate these protocols as part of a daily practice.

The next morning, I awoke at 5:00 AM. I immediately went to my studio and sat among the salt lamps and tiny white lights to experience these beautiful protocols. During the process Teresa's face appeared in my mind. (That's what can happen when you sit in stillness and quiet.) Once again, I felt her energetic pull. I thought to myself, that's it. I need to hold space for Teresa, too, and I resolved to include that as part of my daily practice.

When I was finished with the protocols, I muscle tested some statements to see if I held any resistance about my commitment to my sister. Two issues came up immediately: sadness and doubt.

So often I sit at my vanity and stare at the framed 5x7 of Teresa's beautiful smiling face. If I allow myself to immerse into a deep mental connection with her, I am overtaken by sadness. Memories of our physical lives together erupt, and I miss her intensely. So, I disconnect from her before I can even begin to create, let alone maintain a deeper connection with her Spirit.

Then there's that tiny bit of doubt. That self-talk that says, "Teresa's on to bigger and better experiences with greater purpose."

I quickly did the balances to remove sadness and doubt from my subconscious. Feeling lighter and committed, I knew this time I would follow through.

Shortly after, I was on my way to my yoga class listening to a Lucinda Williams' channel. I felt energized and was in the mood to sing. I began to fast forward to search for a song I knew. Before I could find one, I stopped on Norah Jones' "Humble Me." I didn't know the song, but before I could skip it, I was interrupted by my thoughts (at least I thought they were my thoughts). I remembered the balances I'd done to connect with Teresa. Wanting confirmation that she'd heard me, I yelled over the music, "Hey, Dill! Did you hear me before? Can you give me a sign?"

The second, and I do mean the very second after the word 'sign' left my lips, I clearly heard the song's lyric coming through my speakers.

'Teresa.'

How's that for a calling card?

Stay tuned.

Acknowledgements

There are many people I'd like to thank for their role in supporting the creation of this book. Here they are, and in no special order:

Abigail Rockwell, you really kicked this book into high gear. Thank you, my dear friend, for trusting Spirit, your beautiful brain, profound encouragement and guidance.

Thanks to my brother Patrick and friends Kathy Strom and Deborah Dutko for their collective feedback. You were all invaluable in helping me shape the second draft. It was only after I sent the manuscript to the group that I realized it was June 8th. Grammy's day, of course.

Zito, you've been my muse and my creative partner for more than half my life. You hold a lot of real estate in my heart. Thank you for always jumping at the chance to play a part in my life and in my creativity.

Thank you to authors and writing coaches, and teachers at Sarah Lawrence College, Alexandra Soiseth, and Marcia Bradley, author of *The Home for Wayward Girls*. Your collective brilliance elevated my writing, and your kindness made me feel like I deserved a seat at the table.

Marcia, thank you for all the advice and support you gave freely, and the many emails you answered. I would have been lost without you. Your guidance gave me the permission I needed to discover my own style and have confidence in my voice. You schooled me in book publishing, and because of that I was able to make an informed decision that self-publishing was right for me. Marcia. Marcia. Marcia! You know I am eternally grateful for your guidance.

Sarah Smith Foster of Oxford Blooms Flower Farm, I will hold you personally responsible for getting me out in front of people with my manuscript. Thank for believing in me and in our event, and for hosting such a memorable evening. You are truly a kindred spirit.

Thank you, Kellee White, spiritual medium, psychotherapist and author of her recently released memoir, *Cracked Opened*. You were eager to read my manuscript and offer your endorsement. You encouraged me to self-publish. We barely know each other, and yet you were there for me in spades. Thank you, Kellee, for your help and kindness, and for introducing me to your marketing guru, Michelle Sample, of 5280 Branding.

Michelle, I cannot begin to thank you for everything you've done to prepare me to step out on the world's stage. My new website is gorgeous! You're the busiest person I know, yet you are always there when I need you. We've only just begun working together, and I am already forever grateful for your generosity and for helping me steer this ship. With you onboard, I know Teresa and I can reach the masses.

Thank you, James Van Praagh, for taking time from your busy schedule to review my manuscript and provide me with your special endorsement. You'll never know how much that means to me. I am forever grateful.

Thank you, Deborah Dutko, for helping me layout and format the book cover, and reminding me about all the things I needed to do. You are always so wonderful to work with. Your expertise and guidance has been invaluable. You have been a shining light in my life for the last 30 years, especially since Teresa's death. And you always seem to pass on the perfect wisdom to me at the very moment I need it.

Special thanks to Charlene Chairo, a long-time childhood friend of Teresa's and now one of my closest friends, and another marketing guru who helped me set-up my business back in 2017. Char, you told me from the beginning, "Just publish it yourself, Annie!" You were right, again! Thanks for the many hours you've spent encouraging me, and your constant advice on how to get out and talk about my mission and my book. You have been my biggest cheerleader.

Thank you, Bruce Lipton, for your research that changed my life. I was so grateful to meet you in The Village this past summer during your world tour. Your lectures confirm what I've believed for so long about God and Science and injected me with renewed excitement to get out there and talk boldly about my mission. Your kindness is appreciated by me and PSYCH-K Facilitators and Instructors around the globe, as well as your efforts to awaken humanity and create a peaceful planet. Bruce, do you have any idea how many people reach out to me brimming with eagerness to schedule a session because they saw or read *The Biology of Belief*?

And to the late Rob Williams, originator of PSYCH-K who sadly transitioned too young, and while my book was out for final copy editing. There are no words to thank this outrageously beautiful soul for sharing the sacred gift of PSYCH-K with humanity, and for the hundreds of thousands who have reclaimed their power to create the life they want, and the millions more to come. The world has lost a most extraordinary man, a true visionary in this space committed to elevating humanity to its greatest potential, and who was undoubtedly called home to support this planet from the other side during these trying times. I came so close to meeting you in this lifetime, dear Rob, and look forward to meeting you in the next.

To all of my friends and family who encouraged me along the way and assured me I would finish this book. And for all the times I made you sit down and listen to me read a section aloud. Thank you for believing in me. Every ounce of your support has meant the world to me.

To my mother, truly the most blessed and darling mother I could ever have chosen. Mom, at 84 years old, you are at every one of my events you can possibly attend. Thank you for always being there for me. From as far back as forever, you've been my biggest support, championing every endeavor I've attempted. You have always believed in me. From the time I was born, you've told me I could do anything, that I was beautiful, brilliant, and special—such positive, subconscious downloads. Teresa said it first, and I second it; I believe with all my heart that I'm everything I am because you love me.

My dear sister, Teresa, it's been oh so bittersweet bringing you back to life. How I belly-laughed and cried from my soul while reliving our time together, blissfully ignorant of how hard it would be to let you go again. Thank you, my beautiful girl, for never leaving my side, leading me to our mission and to the work that truly saved my life. Together, I hope we can help bring healing and peace to this planet. I know you will be first in line when I exit this existence. I can see your big smile and open arms. I can feel your intensity. And I can hear you saying,

"We did it, Dill. Welcome home."

Resources

PODCASTS

Fox, Ethann, host. "The Age Of Aquarius|Ethann Fox." Awake and Empowered TV, 6 October 2018

Fox, Ethann, host. "The Age Of Illumination|Patricia Cori." Awake and Empowered TV, 17 March 2018

Fox, Ethann, host. "At the Awake and Empowered Expo! James Gilliland|Marina Jacobi." Awake and Empowered TV, 9 April 2016

Fox, Ethann, host. "Becoming Coherent With The Whole Self| Natalie Sudman." Awake and Empowered TV, 26 August 2017

Fox, Ethann, host. "The Children Of Tomorrow | Mary Rodwell." Awake and Empowered TV, 1 July 2017

Fox, Ethann, host. "Connecting to Source | Caroline Cory." Awake and Empowered TV, 13 May 2017

Fox, Ethann, host. "Crystalline Unity Consciousness|Sandra Walter." Awake and Empowered TV, 23 December 2017

Fox, Ethann, host. "Cymatics|A Portal To The Stars|Mandara Cromwell." Awake and Empowered TV, 7 March 2020

Fox, Ethann, host. "The Days And Nights Of Brahma|Michael Cremo."Awake and Empowered TV, 20 May 2017

Fox, Ethann, host. "Energy Transfer, Awakening To A New Reality|Ethann Fox." Awake and Empowered TV, 14 May 2016

Fox, Ethann, host. "Ethann Fox talks to Dr. Robert Schoch." Awake and Empowered TV, 1 November 2016

Fox, Ethann, host. "Evidence Of Extraterrestrial Communication|Barbara Lamb." Awake and Empowered TV, 10 March 2018

Fox, Ethann, host. "A Fifth Dimensional Life|Anaiis Salles." Awake and Empowered TV, 4 April 2017

Fox, Ethann, host. "Future Human Timelines|Wieteke Koolhof." Awake and Empowered TV, 10 June 2017

Fox, Ethann, host. "The Halls Of Amenti|Billy Carson." Awake and Empowered TV, 26 May 2018

Fox, Ethann, host. "The Human Aura And Energy Circles| Barbara Morey." Awake and Empowered TV, 13 January 2018, https://youtube/EJrmtcfh2TQ?si=f4ZzNg78Du22UOBK

Fox, Ethann, host. "Living 5th Dimensionally In A 3D World| Ethann Fox." Awake and Empowered TV, 13 July 2019

Fox, Ethann, host. "Living Your Planetary Purpose|Ethann Fox." Awake and Empowered TV, 28 January 2017

Fox, Ethann, host. "Our Holographic Reality|Micheila Sheldan." Awake and Empowered TV, 18 March 2017

Fox, Ethann, host. "Pranic Living|Akahi Ricardo." Awake and Empowered TV, 30 January 2016

Fox, Ethann, host. "Pure Synchronism|Darryl Anka." Awake and Empowered TV, 2 December 2017

Fox, Ethann, host. "Relationships And Your Mission|Ethann Fox." Awake and Empowered TV, 25 February 2017

Fox, Ethann, host. "Remote Viewing The Mysteries From High Strangeness To The Self|John Vivanco." Awake and Empowered TV, 1 August 2020

Fox, Ethann, host. "Soul Alchemy|Veronica Avelin." Awake and Empowered TV, 4 May 2019

Fox, Ethann, host. "Soul Essence Activation|Xane Daniel." Awake and Empowered TV, 30 March 2019

Fox, Ethann, host. "The Soul's Journey|Barbara Lamb." Awake and Empowered TV, 3 September 2016

Fox, Ethann, host. "The Tribe Of Many Colors|Kiesha Crowther. " Awake and Empowered TV, 28 April 2018

Fox, Ethann, host. "Vibrational Genetics |Jeilene Tracey." Awake and Empowered TV, 16 June 2018

Fox, Ethann, host. "Vibrational Sound Healing|Mark Romero." Awake and Empowered TV, 11 April 2015

BOOKS:

Anderson, Andrew. Life Between Heaven and Earth: What You Didn't Know About the World Hereafter and How It Can Help You, Harmony, 2016.

Browne, Sylvia. Journey of the Soul Series, Book I: God, Creation, and Tools for Life, Hay House LLC, 1999.

Cannon, Dolores. Conversations with Nostradamus, Volume I, Ozark Mountain Publishing, 1992.

Cannon, Dolores. The Convoluted Universe Book 1, Ozark Mountain Publishing, 2001.

Cannon, Dolores. The Convoluted Universe Book 2, Ozark Mountain Publishing, 2007.

Cannon, Dolores. The Custodians: Beyond Abduction, Ozark Mountain Publishing, 1997.

Cannon, Dolores. Jesus and the Essenes, Ozark Mountain Publishing, 1999.

Cannon, Dolores. Keepers of the Garden, Ozark Mountain Publishing, 1993.

Cannon, Dolores. They Walked with Jesus: Past Life Experiences with Christ, Ozark Mountain Publishing, 2011.

Clark, Ann J., PhD, Joy, Karen, Selinske, Joanne, PhD, & Hargreaves, Marilyn. Wisdom of Souls: Case Studies of Life Between Lives from the Michael Newton Institute, Llewellyn Publications, 2019.

Dillard, Sherry. I'm Still with You: Communicate, Heal & Evolve with Your Loved One on the Other Side, Llewellyn Publications, 2020.

Herman, Bart D. Misquoting Jesus: The Story Behind Who Changed the Bible and Why, HarperOne, San Francisco, 2004.

Jackson, Laura Lynne. The Light Between Us: Stories from Heaven. Lessons for the Living, The Dial Press, 2016.

Jackson, Laura Lynne. Signs: The Secret Language of the Universe, The Dial Press, 2019.

Lipton, Bruce H., PhD. The Biology of Belief: Unleashing the Power of Consciousness, Matter & Miracles, Hay House, 2007.

Moorjani, Anita. Dying to be Me: My Journey from Cancer, to Near Death, to True Healing, Hay House LLC, 2011.

Myss, Caroline, PhD. *Advanced Energy Anatomy*, Sounds True Inc., 2000.

Myss, Caroline, PhD. Anatomy of the Spirit: The Seven Stages of Power and Healing, Three Rivers Press, 1995.

Myss, Caroline, PhD. Channeling Grace: Invoking the Power of the Divine, Sounds True Inc., 2008.

Myss, Caroline, PhD. Energy Anatomy: The Science of Personal Power, Spirituality, and Health, Sounds True Inc., 1996.

Myss, Caroline, PhD. Navigating Hope: How to Turn Life's Challenges into a Journey of Transformation, Sounds True Inc., 2010.

Myss, Caroline, PhD. Sacred Contracts: Awakening Your Divine Potential, Bantam Books, 2000.

Myss, Caroline, PhD. Your Creative Soul: Expressing Your Authentic Voice, Sounds True Inc., 2014.

Phillipps, Bill. Expect the Unexpected: Bringing Peace, Healing, and Hope from the Other Side, New World Library, 2015.

Shealy, MD PhD, C. Norman. Living Bliss: Major Discoveries Along the Holistic Path, Hay House LLC 2014.

Tolle, Eckhart. *A New Earth: Awakening to Your Life's Purpose,* Penguin, 2008.

Van Praagh, James. Ghosts Among Us: Uncovering the Truth About the Other Side, Rider & Co., 2007.

Van Praagh, James. Heaven and Earth: Making the Psychic Connection, Simon & Schuster, 2001.

Van Praagh, James. Talking to Heaven: A Medium's Message of Life After Death, Dutton Adult, 1997.

Weigel, Jennifer. Stay Tuned: Conversations with Dad from the Other Side, Hampton Roads Publishing, 2007.

Weigel, Jennifer. Psychics, Healers and Mediums: A Journalist, a Road Trip, and Voices from the Other Side, Hampton Roads Publishing, 2017.

Weiss, Brian L., MD. Many Lives, Many Masters: The True Story of a Prominent Psychiatrist, His Young Patient, and the Past-Life Therapy That Changed Both Their Lives, Piatkus Books, 1993.

Weiss, Brian L., MD. Same Soul, Many Bodies: Discover the Healing Power of Future Lives through Progression Therapy, Piatkus Books, 2003.

Williams, Robert M. PSYCH-K®: The Missing Peace in Your Life, Spirit, 2000, 2001.

Young, David. The True Story of Jesus and His Wife Mary Magdalena: Their Untold Truth Through Art and Evidential Channeling, Waterside Productions, 2019.

About the Author

Annie Lisa, Transformational Speaker, Lightworker, Spiritual Teacher and Author, was born and raised in the Naugatuck Valley region of Connecticut. In 1996 she graduated Magna Cum Laude with a BA in English from Albertus Magnus College in New Haven. Alongside Annie's 25-year career in marketing and advertising, she was inspired by profound, mystical experiences that began in her late twenties. Annie has dedicated herself to research in the realm of human existence, expanding consciousness and quantum physics.

After the 2015 murder of her sister, Dr. Teresa Sievers, Annie received messages from her departed sister that set her on a journey to discover the transformative work she does today with the subconscious. In 2017 Annie opened her own practice, Divining Your Life. Through client sessions, she has helped hundreds of people break subconscious patterns that have kept them from living the lives they want. Her mission is to awaken humanity to their divine birthright as conscious creators so they can create the life they want, and a world we all want to live in. Annie resides in Connecticut.

www.ingramcontent.com/pod-product-compliance
Lightning Source LLC
Chambersburg PA
CBHW021219130626
46554CB00004B/1288